The Welland Canals
THE GROWTH OF MR. MERRITT'S DITCH

The Welland Canals

THE GROWTH OF MR. MERRITT'S DITCH

Roberta M. Styran
and Robert R. Taylor

with JOHN N. JACKSON

The Flight Locks, Thorold, ca. 1980: *The great achievement and continuing attraction of the Fourth Welland Canal is the double set of three locks which "climb the mountain" of the Niagara Escarpment: a triumph of modern engineering. Yet ever since 1824 the construction and maintenance of all four canals has been a saga of human ingenuity, daring and tragedy. Our pictures reveal how one man's "crotchet" or "folly" (to use 19th-century terms) succeeded against considerable odds and became a vital part of the North American heartland's life line to the sea.* St. Lawrence Seaway Authority: Western Region

CANADIAN CATALOGUING IN PUBLICATION DATA

Styran, Roberta McAfee, 1927–
    The Welland Canals

Bibliography: p.
Includes index.
ISBN 0-919783-63-5

1. Welland Canal (Ont.) – History. I. Taylor,
Robert R., 1939–   . II. Jackson, John N.,
1925–   . III. Title.

HE401.W45S88 1988   386'.47'0971338   C88-093710-6

© Roberta M. Styran & Robert R. Taylor

Edited by Noel Hudson
Cover designed by Gill Stead
Typeset by Linotext, Toronto
Printed by Ampersand, Guelph

Published by:
THE BOSTON MILLS PRESS
132 Main Street
Erin, Ontario
N0B 1T0
(519) 833-2407

American Association
for State and Local History
Award of Merit

Winners of the
Heritage Canada
Communications Award

We wish to acknowledge the financial assistance and encouragement of The Canada Council, the Ontario Arts Council and the Office of the Secretary of State.

CONTENTS

Frontispiece — ii

Acknowledgements — vi

Foreword — vii

Preface — ix

Introduction — xiii

  1. Men With Ideas — 19

  2. Overcoming the Physical Problems — 31

  3. Men With Machines — 43

  4. Industry and Trade — 57

  5. Ships and Shipbuilding — 71

  6. Creating Employment — 85

  7. Creating Communities — 99

  8. People and Pleasures — 113

  9. Difficulties and Disasters — 127

  10. Transforming the Landscape — 139

Afterword: The Future of the Past — 153

Appendix — 159

Abbreviations — 160

Notes — 161

Bibliography — 163

Index — 164

ACKNOWLEDGEMENTS

We are greatly indebted to Robert F. Legget and Wesley B. Turner who read our manuscript in its rough draft and made invaluable suggestions and criticisms, and to John Burtniak, who undertook the same task, and who generously allowed us to make use of his extensive and valuable postcard collection. We were also well served by J.N. Bascom, Arden Phair and Heather Ott, who each read and commented on various individual chapters. Of course, any errors which survive are not their responsibility.

Scores of individuals in three countries offered us assistance and encouragement over five years of research. They include: Emerson Banks, Robert Shipley and the staff, Welland Canals Society; John H. Boyes (London, England); Douglas Burr, Port Dalhousie Quorum; John Cairns; Malcolm Campbell, Bruce McLeod, and the St. Lawrence Seaway Authority (Western Region); A.J. (Tony) Conder, curator, The National Waterways Museum (Gloucester, England); Jane Davies, and the staff, Welland Historical Museum; Brian Dunnigan, curator, Old Fort Niagara (Youngstown, New York); Colin Duquemin, St. Johns Outdoor Studies Centre; Loris Gasparotto, cartographer, Department of Geography, Brock University; Philip H. Grace (Malpas, England); William Koudys; Divino Mucciante, Instructional Media Centre, Brock University; Heather Ott, Pat Schofield and the staff, Port Colborne Marine and Historical Museum; Alex Ormston; John Powell, Ironbridge Gorge Museum (Ironbridge, England); Arden Phair, curator, and the staff, St. Catharines Historical Museum; George Pepper; the late Francis Petrie; Alfred Sagon-King; Fritz vom Scheidt; Olga Slachta, Map Library, Brock University; M.J. Sparrow; Sheila Wilson, formerly Special Collections librarian (who also prepared the Index) and the staff, St. Catharines Centennial Library.

Many others helped without knowing the identity of those mad, inquisitive canal buffs, and unfortunately they too remain anonymous. Their kind assistance, however, was encountered at or through the following organizations: The British Waterways Board, England; Canadian Canal Society, St. Catharines, Ontario; The Inland Waterways Association, London, England; The Ironbridge Gorge Museum Trust (several locations); Metropolitan Toronto Reference Library; Ontario Archives, Toronto, Ontario; National Archives of Canada (formerly Public Archives of Canada), Ottawa, Ontario; Thorold Public Library; Welland Public Library.

Every effort has been made to obtain permission for use of visual materials. If any copyright holder has been overlooked, we will be pleased to make the necessary arrangements for acknowledgement.

We are grateful to the Social Sciences and Humanities Research Council, the Ontario Arts Council, and the Ontario Heritage Foundation for their generous assistance in support of the photographic research necessary for this book.

And last but by no means least, our gratitude to Anne Taylor for services well above and beyond the call of matrimonial duty!

FOREWORD

The Welland Canal of today is one of the very few great ship canals of the world. It is the fourth to link lakes Erie and Ontario on approximately the same route. Now that it is a vital part of the St. Lawrence Seaway, it is being used close to its full capacity, consideration already being given to ways in which this may be increased. And yet it is still but little known to most Canadians.

This fine book will help to correct a rather disturbing neglect. The essential facts about the four successive canals are all here, succinctly and accurately reported. The illustrations, however, make this volume unique. How the authors managed to find and assemble such a wide-ranging and splendid pictorial record is beyond my imagining (and I have had a little experience with similar searches). I find myself fascinated by the vivid appreciation of the steady growth of the Welland Canal from the small venture opened in 1829, which the illustrations so interestingly depict.

As younger Canadians look at the older pictures in this remarkable collection, they will be tempted to think that they represent a world of "long ago and far away." Let me illustrate in a personal way how relatively recent the entire history of the Canal really is — as is indeed the history of Canada itself. When I settled in Ottawa in 1947, I often enjoyed the good company of a valued friend, a fellow engineer, a few years older than myself. He had lived all his life in Ottawa and so had many happy early memories of the capital city. One of these, about which he told me, was attending a garden party in Rockcliffe with his Father. The American Society of Civil Engineers were holding a meeting in Ottawa; the party was to honour one of their past-presidents, a resident of Rockcliffe, Thomas Coltrin Keefer. He was one of the early great men in Canadian engineering; not only had he been president of the A.S.C.E., but he was the founding president of the Canadian Society of Civil Engineers in 1887. At the time of the garden party (1914) he was in his nineties but still active in mind and body. And my friend heard this grand old man tell how, as a little boy, he had stood by the side of the first Welland Canal, his hand in his Father's, as they watched the very first vessels sail through the recently completed canal — this in 1829.

As is the case with most engineering works, once opened and in regular use, each of the Welland Canals ceased to be "news" and thereafter attracted the attention of the media only when trouble developed. In the case of the Fourth Canal, such occasions have been rare indeed — a bridge badly damaged, for example, in 1974, and damage to a lock wall in 1985. This most recent accident unfortunately occurred close to the end of the open season for navigation and so caused trouble with shipping. Correction of both called for emergency construction operations, carried out around the clock with great skill.

Quite the most surprising thing about these few isolated failures has been their infrequency, in view of the varying water levels in every lock many times a day and the frequent use of movable bridges. This is testimony indeed to the excellence of the original designs and construction, as also to the diligent maintenance work carried out unceasingly through the more than fifty years since the Canal was officially opened. Canada, the United States of America, and indeed the world have been well served by the men of the Welland Canal, to whom this volume is a well-deserved tribute.

Robert F. Legget
Ottawa, 31 October 1987

P.1 Thorold, 1882 – Romance vs. Reality: *A charming drawing of Lock 23 (Picturesque Canada, 1882) provides fascinating details, yet leaves the well-informed viewer puzzled. To the right, the land seems to slope away from the height to the left, which is not the case in reality. Also, even allowing for the growth of trees during the past century, it is unlikely that the spire of St. John's Anglican Church could have been seen from this point on the Third Canal. Furthermore, the amount of sail being carried by the schooner would have been unwise, given the thunderclouds blowing up, even if legal. In the event of a squall, the tug would have had a difficult job preventing the schooner from crashing into the gates and possibly flooding a large area. Moral: enjoy the nostalgia and beauty of period drawings, but don't necessarily accept them as accurate representations!* SCHM: N-3678

P.2 The Fourth Canal – Getting the Right Angle: (opposite) *Construction of the Fourth Canal was well documented by photographers[1] who used various devices to capture the action, such as the scaffolding atop a flatcar, shown here, which enabled the cameraman to achieve a spectacular angle. But even such painstaking efforts, concentrating as they did on machinery and not on the men who laboured, do not tell the complete story of the construction of this "technological marvel."* SCHM: N-1283

PREFACE

The best way to understand the saga of the Welland Canals is to investigate their physical remains on foot and to watch the continuing operation of the present canal. Since this is not practical for everyone, we hope that our book will enable the reader to sense the phenomenon of change, in its many dimensions, on the local scene. As well, our images reflect international developments over more than a century and a half.

In contrast to many North American canals, the early phase of the Welland Canal's history was one of private, not governmental, enterprise. The Rideau Canal, for example, begun in 1825, was financed by the British government to provide water transport for British troops and supplies in the event of American invasion. The British military engineers who built the Rideau Canal were trained to produce not only informative charts, but also drawings, many touched up with watercolour, so that the British imperial authorities might be kept in touch with developments. In contrast, since the First Welland Canal was initially financed to a large extent by private Canadian and New York sources, its construction lacked pictorial documentation to accompany the written reports and (very few) charts.

In fact, it was not until the 1880s, during construction of the Third Welland Canal, that artists recorded both the "new" and the "old" (Second) canals for such publications as the *Canadian Illustrated News* and *Picturesque Canada* [Fig. 1].

By the 1880s the camera was also capturing scenes from Port Dalhousie to Port Colborne – a less picturesque record, but far more accurate for the historian's purpose. Even so, photographic records of the actual construction of the Third Canal are rare [see, for example, Chap. 2, Fig. 13]. Perhaps regretting this, the builders of the Fourth (present) Canal saw to it that, during its construction (1913-1932), official photographers recorded all significant sites and occasions along the waterway [Fig. 2]. Indeed, this detailed record has continued: the St. Lawrence Seaway Authority has turned over boxes of past material to the National Archives in Ottawa and maintains an ongoing photographic record.

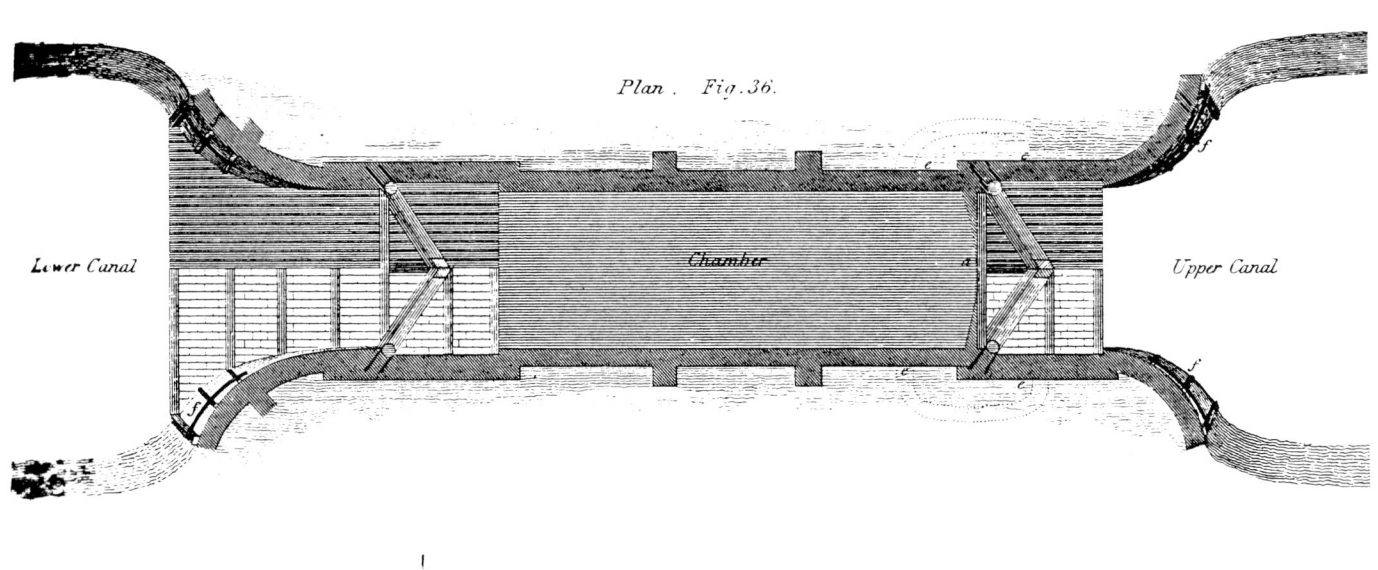

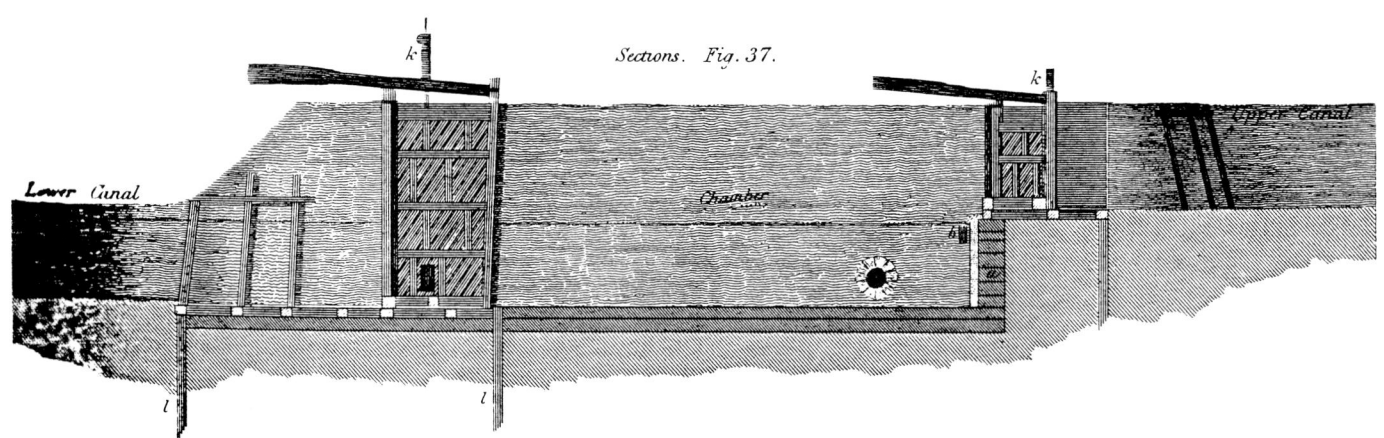

P.3 Lock Plans, ca. 1820: *Drawings such as these from Rees' Cyclopedia would have been known to engineers of the first Welland Canal. Similar drawings, for the Shubenacadie Canal, by Francis Hall [see p. xiii], can be seen in the Public Archives of Nova Scotia. Unfortunately, nothing comparable has survived for the Welland.* Rees, Vol. II plate v

The absence of pictorial records has proved unfortunate for both canal buffs and historians, since the dearth of such graphic materials for the early history of the Welland forces us to rely on verbal descriptions, maps and plans [Fig. 3], and comparative material from the United States and abroad. In some cases we have used 20th-century artists' re-creations based on similar sources [Fig. 4].

Throughout, we have tried to show the history of the canals, and at least some of the people who made and gained from them, over more than a century and a half, in all their diversity. We hope our readers will enjoy this journey back into time as much as we have done in preparing it.

P.4 St. Catharines – a Lock on the First Canal: *This fine pastel drawing, a 20th-century artist's reconstruction, depicts the hand-operated wooden lock gates, a tow-horse, and a schooner with its sails properly reefed for passage through the early canal. But, which lock is represented? Can the scene be accurately dated? See also Introduction, Figure 1, where a re-creation of the passage of the first Canadian ship through the canal poses another problem: the name of the vessel. Contemporary sources refer to her both as the ANNIE AND JANE, and the ANN AND JANE.* Charles Simpson

In.1 The First Passage, 1829: *This artist's re-creation shows the Canadian ANNIE AND JANE at Lock 1 (at the approximate site of Gary Road) in Port Dalhousie, followed by the American B.H. BROUGHTON, as they made the historic first transit of the Welland Canal, from Lake Ontario to Buffalo. The artist has taken considerable licence (not only with the ANNIE AND JANE's name!): it was a bitterly cold day, so few would likely have been seated, and gloves, mufflers and overcoats would probably have been worn. Indeed, ice had to be broken to allow the passage of the vessels. Nevertheless, the indomitable Merritt turned out for the occasion, recording later in his journal that the "ANNIE AND JANE passed by, displaying a number of flags, ensigns and pendants, also a beautiful silk flag with the words 'The King, God Bless Him!' imprinted in gold letters, surmounted by the Crown, erected on her bow. ..."*[2]   SCHM: N-3216

INTRODUCTION: SETTING THE SCENE

The Welland Canal (1824-29) was initiated by local businessmen to stimulate local and regional trade. By the 1840s the canal's importance to the economy of British North America was recognized by government takeover of the privately owned Welland Canal Company in order to finance the urgently needed rebuilding. The locks and channel were enlarged (Second Canal, 1842-45) to accommodate the increasing size of ships. Following Confederation (1867) and the opening of the Canadian West, the waterway was seen as a vital link in a crucial artery of North American trade, and was once again rebuilt and enlarged (Third Canal, 1874-87). By 1913 the ever-larger ships from around the world necessitated yet another reconstruction (Fourth Canal, 1913-32).

These are the bare facts. The history of the Welland Canal is actually a saga of men, money, machines, misery, and daring flights of technological imagination.

The opening of the Welland Canal for the passage of vessels, in November 1829 [Fig. 1], was a remarkable feat: the construction of about 40 miles (64 km) of canal after only 40 years of settlement. United Empire Loyalists (English, Scottish, Germans, Dutch, Irish, and some Blacks) had begun arriving in the Niagara Peninsula in the 1780s, and by the 1820s both population and resources (financial and technical) were still limited. But those settlers had come from already well-established colonies, and were energetic and far-seeing men. In addition, the instigator of the project, William Hamilton Merritt, together with George Keefer and others, was very conscious of the vulnerability of the new settlements to attack from across the nearby border with the United States, since many of them had served in the War of 1812. Finally, these men were aware that they were living in an "Age of Canals."

By 1824, when Merritt's canal actually was begun, the immediate example was the Erie Canal in neighbouring New York State, which had been started in 1817. However, equally important in the minds of these Upper Canadians was the canal network of Great Britain, as we know from many references in both the Welland Canal Company papers and in contemporary newspaper accounts. In 1818, for example, the House of Assembly of Upper Canada, considering possibilities for waterways, requested the Lieutenant-Governor, Sir Peregrine Maitland, to inquire in England regarding "a Civil Engineer of sufficient abilities for the purpose...."[3] The Provincial Agent resident in London subsequently wrote back to Maitland: "After a diligent inquiry I have no hesitation in fixing on John Rennie, Esquire, Civil Engineer, as the most proper person to give me the information required."[4] The Agent passed on two names – Josias Jessop, then serving in Bermuda, and Hamilton Fulton, who had recently proceeded to make a survey in North Carolina – both at the recommendation of Rennie. Neither man was involved with the construction of canals in Canada. However, Francis Hall, asked to report on an 1824 survey for the Welland Canal conducted by American surveyors, was described by George Keefer (president of the Welland Canal Company) as "a scientific educated Engineer (under the celebrated Tilford [sic]) of much practical knowledge, now employed in constructing the Monument at Queenston and the Canal at Burlington Beach."[5] Keefer was referring to Thomas Telford [Fig. 2], responsible for many of Great Britain's canals and for advances in tunnel construction.

Telford's indirect connection, through Francis Hall, with canal construction in the colonies was widespread. Hall was consulted as engineer for the Burlington Bay Canal, constructed in Upper Canada between 1823 and 1826, and prepared surveys for the Shubenacadie and Bras d'Or canals in Nova Scotia, and for the Chignecto Canal in New Brunswick. He was appointed to superintend construction of the Shubenacadie in 1826, and remained in Nova Scotia until funds ran out in

1832. Telford was consulted by Hall, at least in connection with the Shubenacadie, and in fact purchased shares worth a total of £482.16.0.

In addition, when Merritt visited England in the summer of 1828 to raise funds for completion of the Welland, he submitted the plans to Telford, as we know from a letter written by Telford in which he expressed his approval. (Telford also purchased 20 shares, worth £225, in the Welland Canal Company at this time.)

In.2 Thomas Telford (1757-1834): *Telford was also involved in the introduction of iron in the construction of bridges and aqueducts, and is shown here with the world's first iron aqueduct, at Pontcysyllte, in Wales (opened 1805). He had been consulted abroad and spent six weeks in 1808 surveying in Sweden for the location of 58 locks for the Göta Canal. He was also involved in the construction of roads and docks.*

Elton Collection, Ironbridge Gorge Museum Trust

During that same visit to England, Merritt actually visited the first major canal in Britain, that constructed by James Brindley for the Duke of Bridgewater, opened in 1776 [Fig. 3]. This canal allowed barges to load coal in the Duke's underground mines at Worsley for transport directly to Manchester or to the Mersey estuary via a 10-lock flight at Runcorn. Merritt recorded in his journal visits to both Worsley and Runcorn.

Nevertheless, the ultimate inspiration lies in Europe, in the Languedoc area of France where, in 1753, the 17-year-old Duke of Bridgewater had toured the Canal du Midi, the "first modern canal" [Fig. 4]. It was only four years later that the Duke, visiting his Manor House at Worsley, became aware of the canalization of Sankey Brook to carry coal across the Mersey River. The combination of this endeavour and his recollections of the Continental model inspired the Duke to begin his own canals.

In.3 Francis Egerton, 3rd Duke of Bridgewater (1736-1803): *The Duke gestures proudly towards his canal, where we see not only two groups of towboys hard at work, but also the famous stone aqueduct carrying the canal over the Irwell River at Barton. An anonymous writer said of the Duke's engineer, James Brindley, that his work was "truly astonishing. At Barton bridge he has erected a navigable canal in the air; for it is as high as the tops of trees"*[6] *(200 yards long, 38 feet above the river).* A Contemporary Print

In.4 Staircase Locks on the Canal du Midi: *A flight of seven staircase locks was built between 1666 and 1681 at Béziers on the Canal du Midi. The 150-mile-long (241 km) waterway, from the River Garonne near Toulouse to the Etang de Thau near Sète, linked the Atlantic and Mediterranean.*   David & Charles Publishers

Even the Canal du Midi (completed 1681) was itself not the first canal in the Languedoc: an earlier one, begun in 1604, under the patronage of Henry IV and Sully, had been completed in 1642 with the backing of Louis XIV (the "Sun King" was interested in a 1686 proposal for a canal at Chignecto as well!). Canal-building was also taking place in Germany and the Low Countries, and had begun in the United States where, in the 1790s, one or two small canals had been completed in the territory east of the Alleghenies. In 1822 the 22-mile (35 km) Santee Canal, including 12 locks, was opened in South Carolina.

The Santee was built by a private company, as were most of the English canals. But the Champlain Canal (from the Hudson River to Lake Champlain), completed in 1823, and the Erie (from Albany on the Hudson via the Mohawk Valley to Buffalo on Lake Erie, thus connecting the Atlantic to lakes Ontario and Erie) were both financed by the New York State government.

So when Merritt began to plan his canal, there were models for both state and private financing, on both sides of the Atlantic. When initial attempts to have the British or Canadian governments finance his dream failed, Merritt decided to "go it alone" – or at least with the help of area businessmen first, then of investors in Lower Canada and in the United States, primarily in New York City, but also including some of the contractors themselves. By early 1826 the government of Upper Canada had granted a loan of £25,000, and the following year it agreed to purchase stock in the Welland Canal Company worth a further £50,000. In 1826 the British government authorized a grant of 1/9 the estimated cost (which was not paid); then in July 1828 it offered *either* an increased grant (reflecting current estimates) *or* a loan of £50,000. Merritt, on behalf of the Welland Canal Company, chose the loan. Merritt had been authorized to sell stock while in England: the list of shareholders was headed by no less a figure than the Prime Minister, the Duke of Wellington [Fig. 5], who had taken 50 shares.

In.5 Arthur Wellesley, 1st Duke of Wellington (1769-1852): *Britain's "Iron Duke," hero of the Peninsular Wars, sent a "Memorandum on the Defence of Canada" to Lord Bathurst (March 1819), in which he strongly advocated construction of an Ottawa – Rideau communications system. He also noted that "All these lines of [water] communication ought to be rendered, if possible, so perfect as that a steam-vessel might be used to tow the loaded boats."*[7]

Sir T.A. Lawrence, Victoria and Albert Museum

Wellington had been appointed Master-General of the Ordnance in 1819, responsible for both the supply of guns, munitions and supplies, and the supervision of fortifications for all British military establishments. He was keenly interested in the defence of the British colonies in North America, and as early as 1814 had written to Lord Bathurst (Colonial Secretary): "I believe that the defence of Canada…depends upon the navigation of the lakes…. Any offensive operation founded upon Canada must be preceded by the establishment of a naval superiority on the lakes."[8]

"Merritt's Ditch," then, although a personal vision, was an integral part of an international phenomenon — *The Age of Canals!*

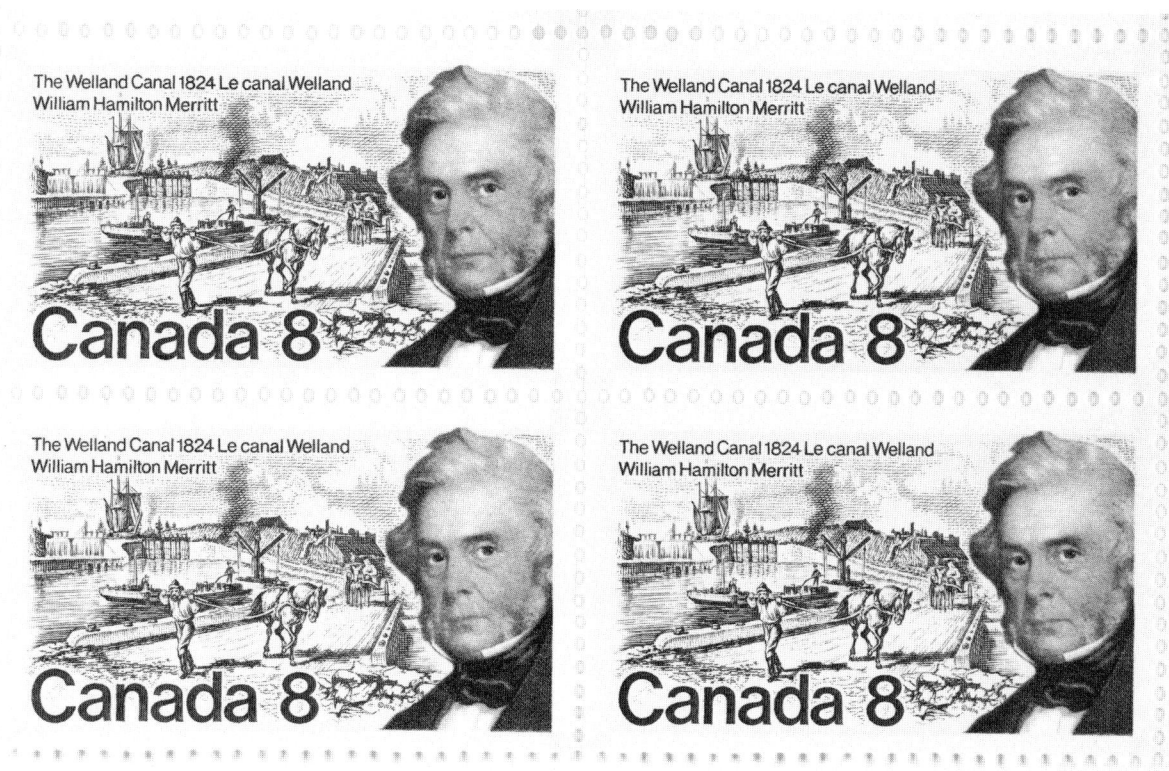

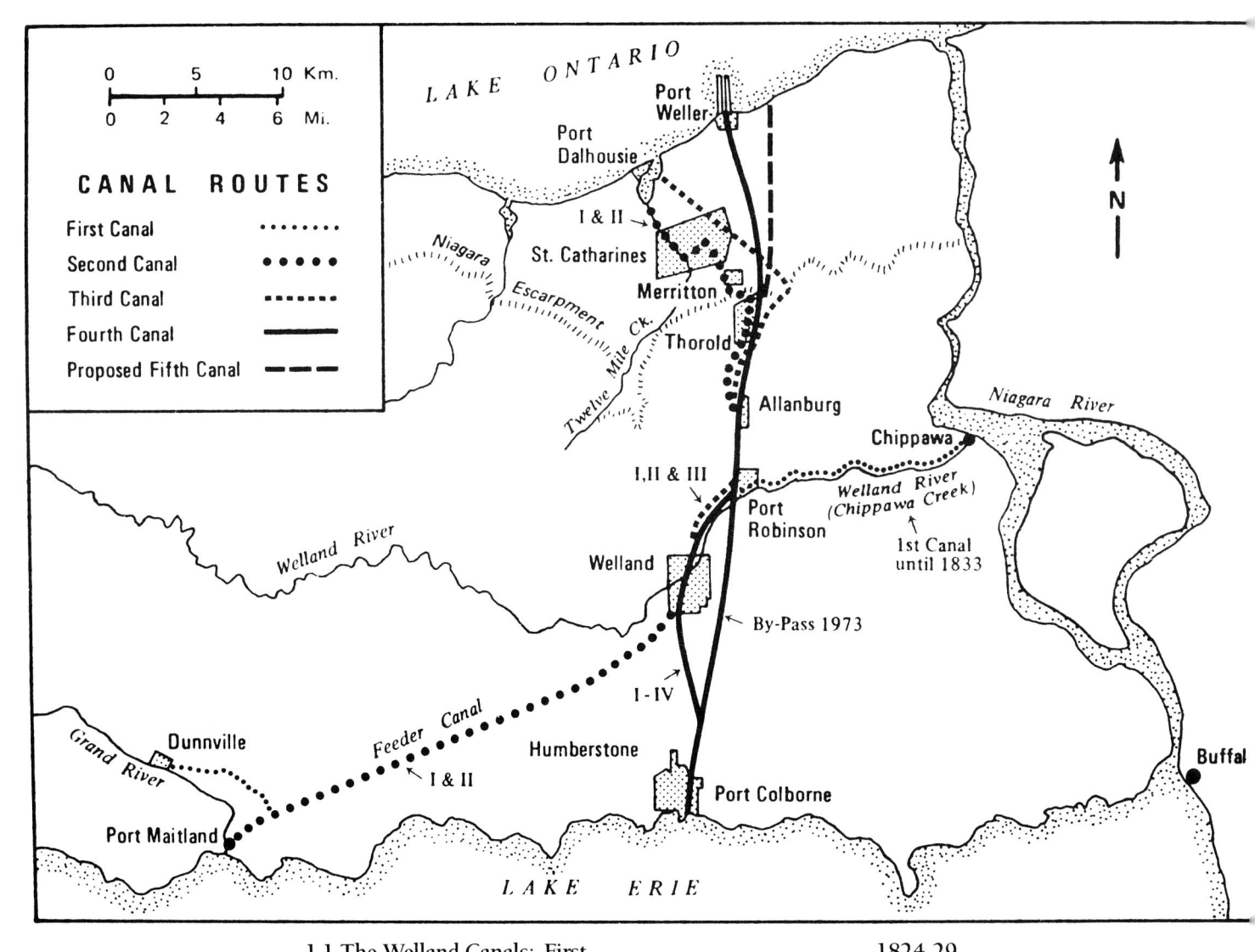

1.1 The Welland Canals:
First	1824-29
Second	1842-45
Third	1874-87
Fourth	1913-32
Welland By-Pass	1965-73

Loris Gasparotto, Department of Geography, Brock University

1. MEN WITH IDEAS

The Welland Canal is now part of some 2,350 miles (3,780 km) of international waterway linking the Atlantic Ocean with the heartland of North America. As with so many great endeavours, it had an apparently insignificant beginning. The "acorn" from which this impressive economic lifeline grew was limited and local: the need for a steady supply of water to power the saw and flour mills belonging to William Hamilton Merritt [Fig. 2] and some of his friends and neighbours along Twelve Mile Creek in St. Catharines, Ontario. Two branches of this stream run over the crest of the Niagara Escarpment, join at its foot, and flow northward to Lake Ontario approximately 12 miles (19 km) west of the Niagara River, hence "Twelve Mile" Creek. However, the creek did not provide a steady source of water power. Millers suffered from too much during spring freshets and too little during the summer dry months.

William Hamilton Merritt was a hard-working, humourless visionary who by 1818 owned a large house and general store in St. Catharines, and a farm and mill-site on Twelve Mile Creek. Here he had built a mill-dam, saw- and flour mills, a distillery, cooper shop, smithy, and five houses to accommodate workers. He had also drilled two shafts to obtain salt. Unfortunately, profitable operation of the mills was threatened by the creek's irregular flow.

1.2 William Hamilton Merritt (1793-1862): *This portrait (probably about 1860) suggests more a man of tough-minded ambition and determination to succeed than an entrepreneur of considerable vision and imagination. When Merritt was in England (May 1828) to raise funds for the completion of the canal, he tried several times to see the editor of the London Times, to no avail. Finally, when Merritt was told he could have five minutes of the editor's time, he spread out a map on the desk and said: "Here is Lake Erie – here is the Falls of Niagara – this is Lake Ontario – and this, the St. Lawrence, and the Atlantic: and here is the route of the great Welland Canal."[9] The editor thereupon agreed to publicize Merritt's plans, thus providing a powerful boost to the attempt to raise funds in Britain.* SCHM: N-4101

Merritt's original problem was common to other businessmen of what is now the St. Catharines-Thorold area [Fig. 3]. Of the eight men named as provisional directors of the nascent Welland Canal Company in a charter of 19 January 1824, six were personal friends of Merritt's. They included George Keefer [Fig. 4], like Merritt, a storekeeper and mill-owner; John DeCew, whose mills were large [Fig. 5] and whose influence was considerable; and George Adams (brother of Thomas, whose mill Merritt had bought in 1815), also a mill-owner on Twelve Mile Creek. Keefer and DeCew operated in Thorold; Adams, lower down on the creek. In addition, William Chisholm (a St. Catharines store-owner), Paul Shipman (who operated a tavern where the Niagara-Burlington Bay road crossed the creek), Thomas Merritt (father of William Hamilton), and one Joseph Smith (about whom nothing is known) were also keen to ensure a reliable source of water power [Fig. 6].

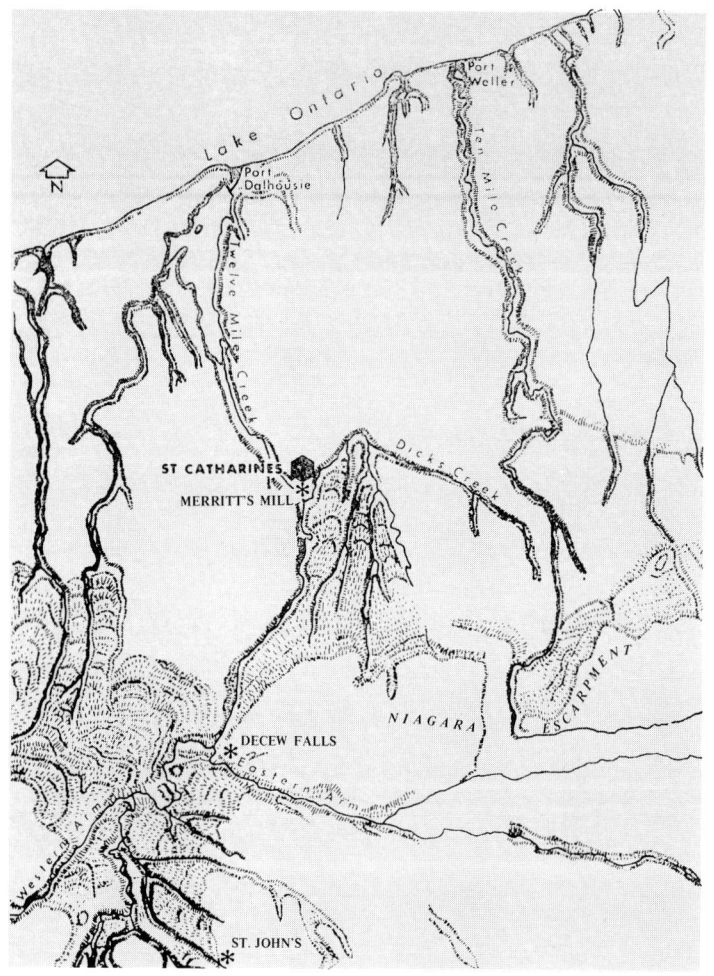

1.3 Where the Idea was Born, ca. 1820: *In the northeast corner of the Niagara Peninsula, a score of streams pour into the branches of Twelve Mile Creek, providing exploitable but unreliable water power. These watercourses also offer channels for canal-builders: Twelve Mile and Dick's Creek for the first two Welland Canals; Ten Mile Creek for the Fourth (present) Canal.* Map Library, Brock University, retouched by Loris Gasparotto, Dept. of Geography

1.4 George Keefer (1773-1858) (opposite, top left): *Of Alsatian background, he emigrated to Upper Canada from New Jersey in 1792, securing a 600-acre (ca. 243 hectares) tract of land above the Niagara Escarpment, in the area later known as Thorold. Like Merritt, a mill-owner (he built his first mill in Thorold, in the middle of the woods, before the canal went through), Keefer became the first president of the Welland Canal Company. He founded a dynasty of engineers, the most notable of whom was his twelfth son, Thomas Coltrin Keefer (see Chap. 3).* PAC: PA-134907

1.5 DeCew Falls, 1875 (opposite, top right): *Where the waters of the eastern branch of Twelve Mile Creek fall over the Niagara Escarpment was an ideal site for milling, but the flow proved unreliable because of the seasonal rise and fall (as at the site of Merritt's mill). The Escarpment (here rising over 184 feet/56 m) itself would be a continuing challenge to the canal-builders.* Page's Atlas

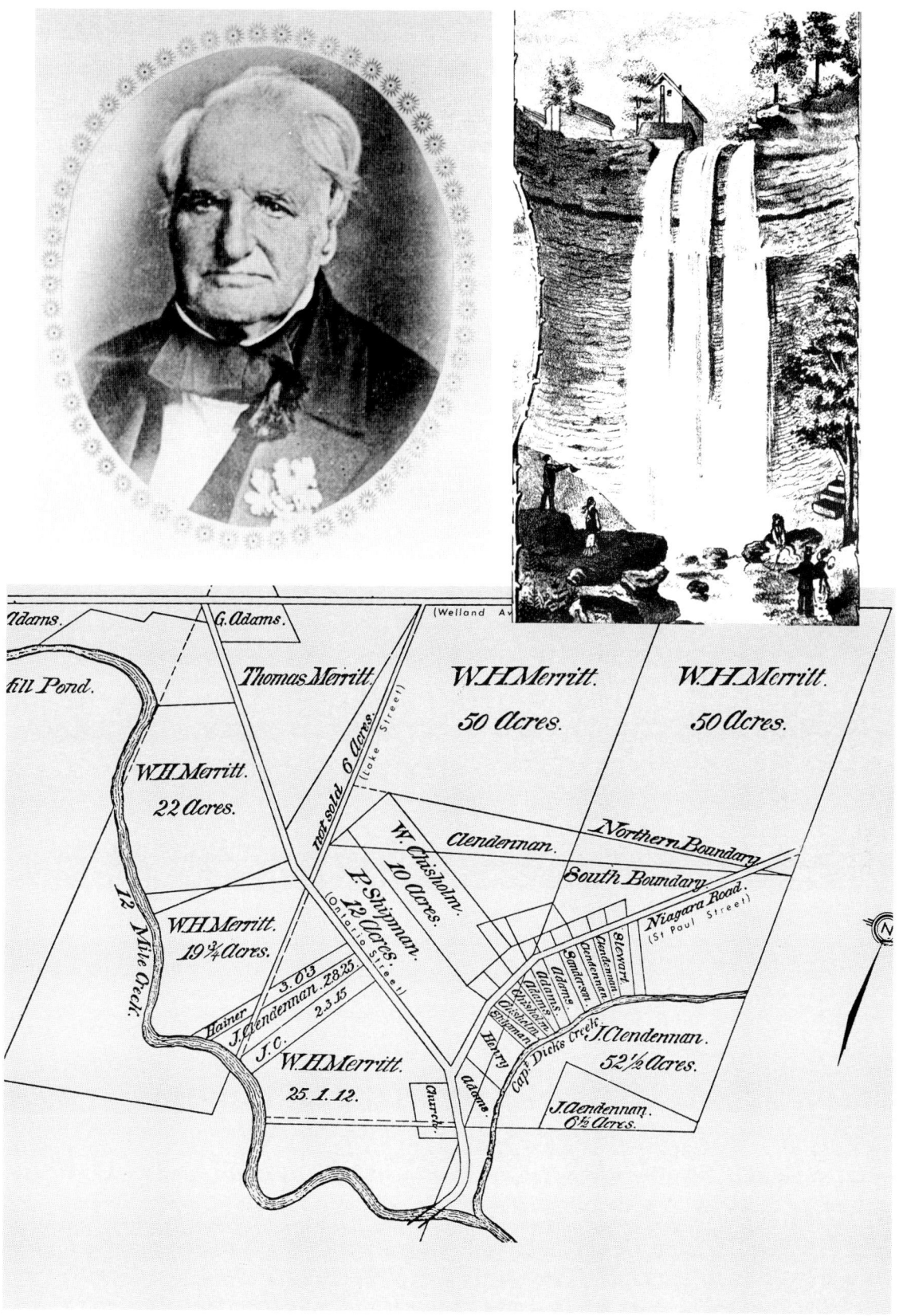

1.6 St. Catharines, ca. 1823: *A legal reconstruction of the growing town shows clearly the prominent position of Merritt as landowner, as well as smaller parcels of land held by his father, Thomas Merritt, and George Adams, Paul Shipman and William Chisholm, other original directors of the Welland Canal Company.*
JNJ, p. 158.

But these men had even more in common. All (except William Hamilton Merritt) were first-generation United Empire Loyalists, and all had had military experience, either in the American Revolution or the War of 1812, or both. They all knew that residents of the Niagara Peninsula had helped to repel the invasion from the United States during 1812-14, and that the military frontier was no further afield than the Niagara River [Fig. 7]. They also knew that when the Erie Canal (begun 4 July 1815) was completed across New York State from Albany to Buffalo, all trade from Upper Canada upstream of Niagara Falls would be directed into the United States and, through Albany, to New York and the Atlantic [Fig. 8].

1.7 The Battle of Queenston Heights, October 13, 1812: *An engraving (based on a painting by Capt. James Dennis) illustrates several stages of the engagement simultaneously. Both the colonial and imperial governments thought that support should be given for a secure, all-British water route between the lakes.*
DeVolpi (*Can. Illust. News*, 1871)

Ironically, despite their awareness of both the military and economic threats, Merritt and his friends had to rely on contractors and workers from the Erie, since even their limited expertise was not available in the settlements of the Niagara Peninsula. On 21 July 1823 William Hamilton Merritt had visited Montezuma, N.Y., and written in his journal: "There is no impediment whatsoever in our plan;...an advantage will be derived for begining [sic] early, as many of the contractors being out of work will have all their tools on hand and prepared to commence immediately...."[10]

An indication of North Americans' relative inexperience in canal-building is that Nathan S. Roberts, referred to by Merritt in July 1823 as the "head engineer" on the Erie Canal at Lockport, had been a schoolteacher who had taught himself simple surveying—after 1816, when he had become involved with the Erie. In the summer of 1824 he was one of several "engineers" asked to submit a report to the Welland Canal Company on two routes for the original canal. The final decision was based on the recommendations of Telford-trained Francis Hall (see Introduction).

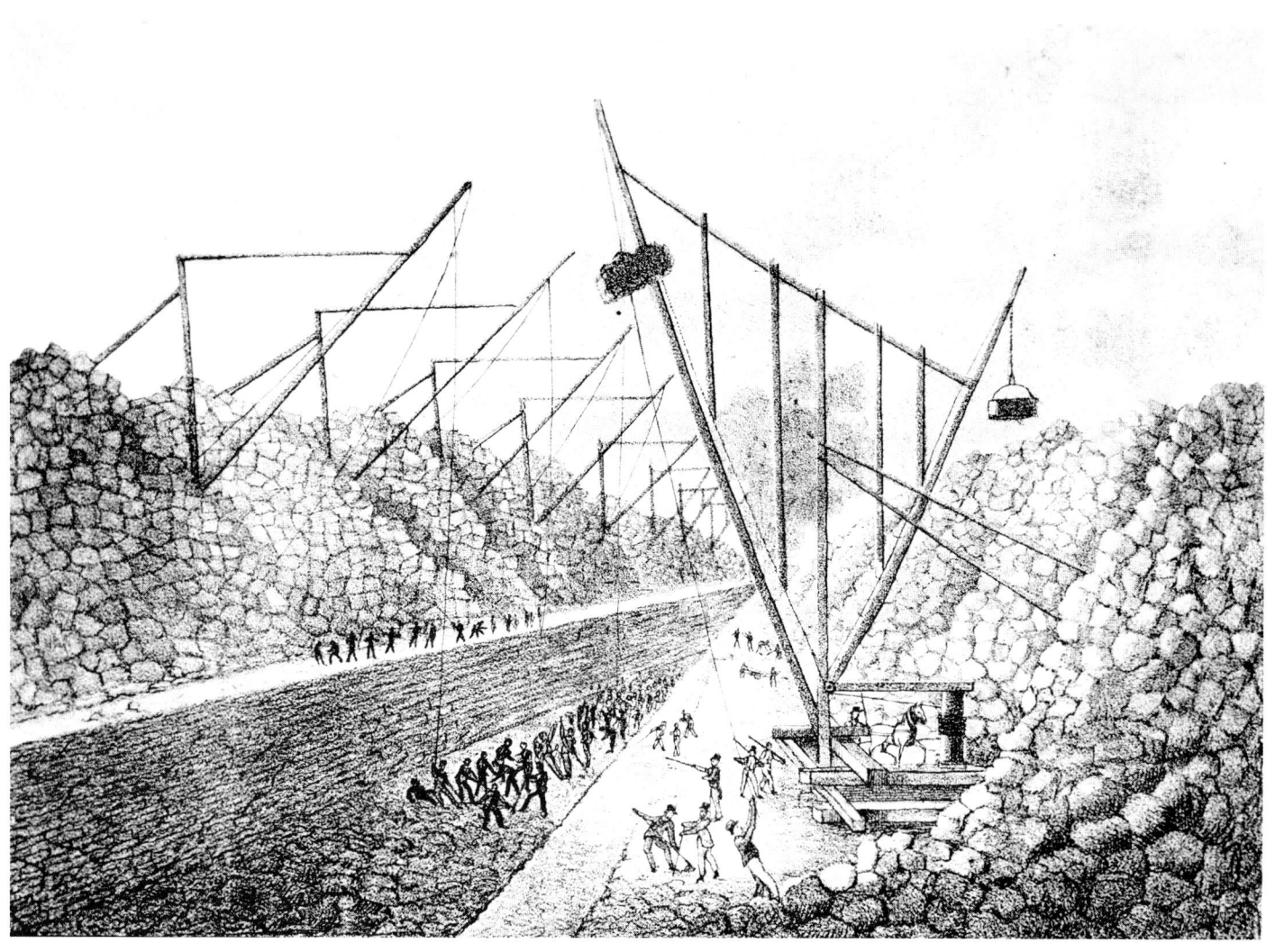

1.8 The Economic Threat from New York State: *Workers slice through the "rock cut" near Lockport, as American "know-how" was put to work building the Erie Canal from 1817 to 1825. It should be noted that even their knowledge was limited and gained "on the job." Note the hard-working horse on the treadmill and the forest of specially designed cranes.* Buffalo and Erie County Historical Society

Another matter of concern to Merritt and his supporters was the threat to Montreal's commercial supremacy, which was based on a monopoly of the St. Lawrence River system, the only northern water route around the Appalachians between the seaboard and the hinterland. The possibility of Montreal's decline concerned business and political interests in both Upper and Lower Canada. And so, while the initial impetus behind plans to build a canal comparable to the Erie, but located on British soil, came from William Hamilton Merritt and his local associates, they soon found support at the highest levels in York (capital of Upper Canada), since the proposed canal would offset the threat of economic, and perhaps subsequent military, aggression by the United States [Fig. 9].

For example, the Earl of Dalhousie, Governor-in-Chief of the Canadas from 1819 to 1828, had been one of Wellington's generals and was aware of the vital importance of improved water communications to the development of the British colonies in North America. In March of 1824 he received Merritt "with every kindness," being "very favourably impressed"[11] with his ideas and promising to bring them before the Home (i.e., British) authorities. (Merritt acknowledged support from the Governor by naming the northern terminus "Port Dalhousie.")

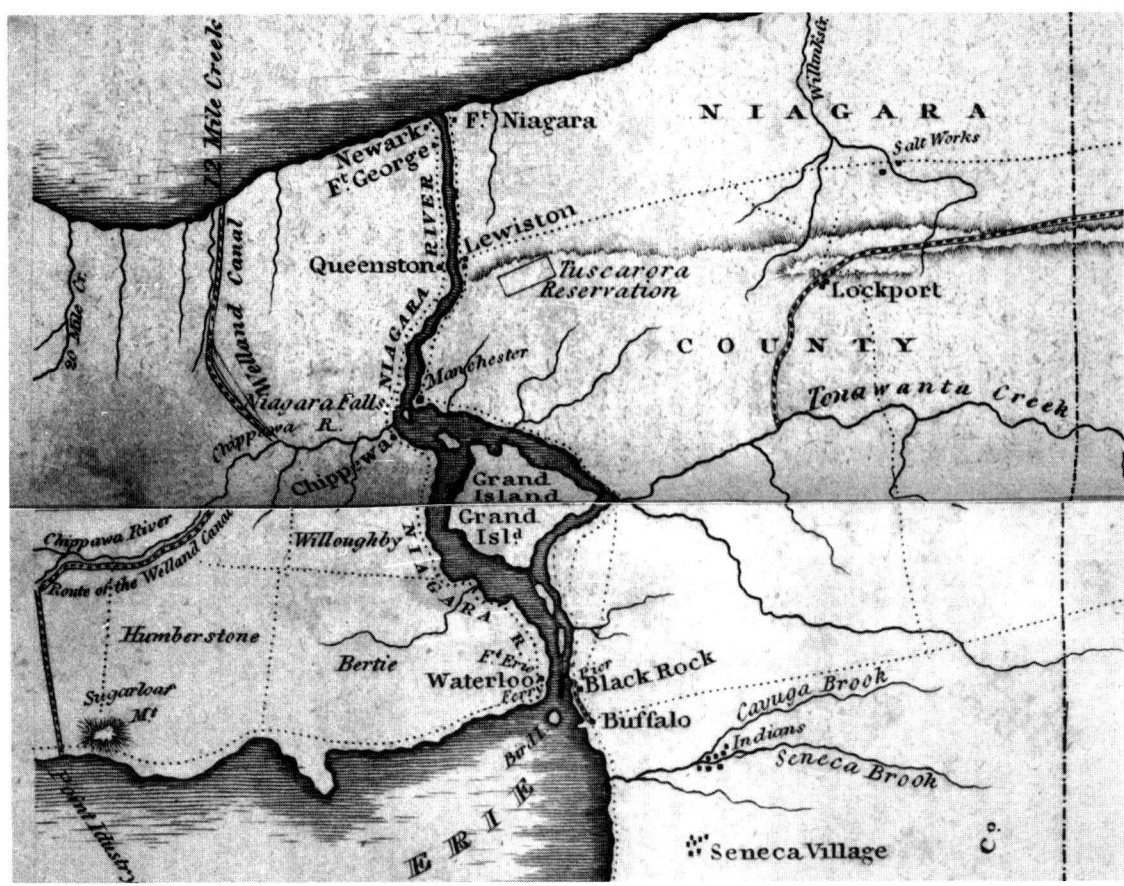

1.9 The Proposed Route of the First Welland Canal, 1826: *Published in conjunction with attempts by the Welland Canal Company to raise money in New York, this map was designed to stimulate American interest in the waterway under construction. It shows the Erie Canal, completed in 1825, and the proposed route of the Welland. The southern extension of Merritt's waterway to Lake Erie was not completed until 1833, and the route of the canal as constructed differed in several respects.* Traveller, pp. 79 and 99

In addition, the successive Lieutenants-Governor of Upper Canada during construction of the canal, Sir Peregrine Maitland (1818-28) and Sir John Colborne (1828-38), both supported the project. Maitland was a firm believer in "improvements" to both land and water communication as a means of attracting immigration and thus increasing prosperity. According to Merritt's son, Maitland "used to visit the canal frequently, bringing his guests to see the works thereon, in which he appeared to take a deep interest;"[12] and in mid-June of 1829, "St. Catharines was visited by the Lieutenant-Governor, who, in company with Mr. Merritt, inspected the works on the Grand River. [Merritt] describes Sir John Colborne [Fig. 10] as a very hard rider…."[13] Again, the naming of Ports Maitland and Colborne acknowledged Merritt's gratitude.

When a new charter had been obtained (late February 1825) for the Welland Canal Company [Fig. 11], naming seven directors, only Merritt and Keefer remained of the original group of merchants and millers in the neighbourhood of "The Twelve." The local people were succeeded by men considerably higher on the social and political ladder: the Honourable John Henry Dunn, Receiver General of Upper Canada; Honourable John Beverley Robinson, Attorney General of Upper Canada [Fig. 12]; William Allan, president of the government-sponsored Bank of Upper Canada; Henry John Boulton, Solicitor General of Upper Canada; D'Arcy Boulton (father of Henry John), a judge of assize; and Colonel Joseph Wells, a member of the Legislative Council. Of these men, Merritt's son was to write: "It cannot be forgotten that the gentlemen in York [Toronto] known as the Family Compact were able and patriotic assistants toward the scheme."[14] Reviled as they were by liberals, men such as Robinson, the Boultons, William Allan and John Strachan (member of the Executive Council 1818-36 and of the Legislative Council 1820-41, and later Bishop of Toronto) were shrewd in their willingness to support the Niagara waterway.

1.10 (Left) **Sir John Colborne (1778-1863)**: *As Lieutenant-Governor he supported Merritt's efforts to raise funds for the canal, guaranteeing a loan of £10,000 in 1829. When the canal was extended from Port Robinson directly to Lake Erie (1833) Merritt named the southern terminus Port Colborne.*   PAC: C-10889

1.12 (Right) **John Beverley Robinson (1791-1863)**: *Attorney General of Upper Canada (1818-29) and Chief Justice (1829-62), he was a director of the Welland Canal Company (1825-28) and was another of the influential men whose support was recognized by Merritt in the naming of canal-spawned communities: Port Robinson (originally known as Port Beverley).*   PAC: C-22381

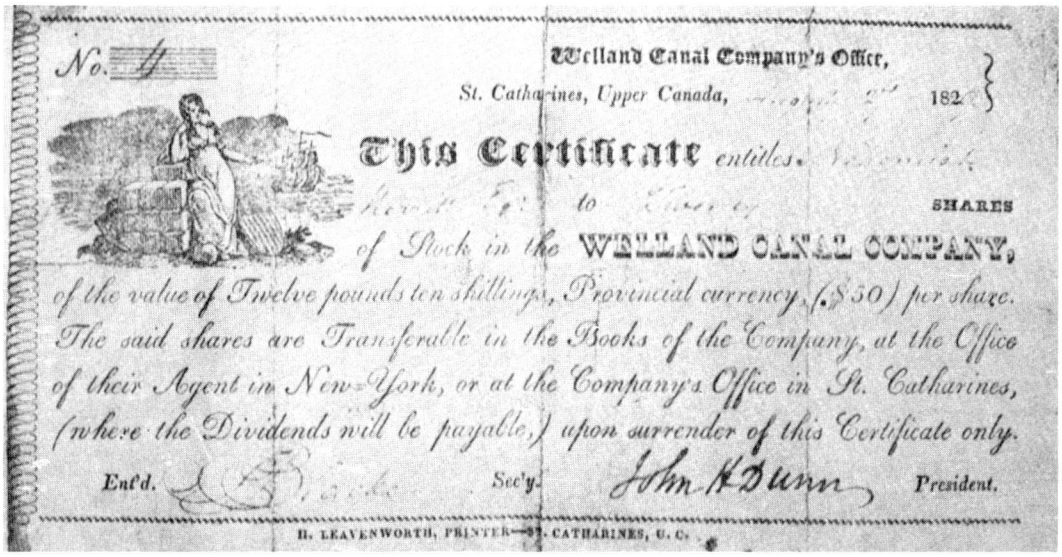

1.11 **A Welland Canal Company Stock Certificate, 1824**: *An observer in 1865 wrote that "a wilder, more ill considered scheme than the one originally put forth, one showing more ignorance and recklessness on the part of the projectors, it is scarcely possible to conceive."[15] Nevertheless, investors were found and the company — and the canal — was launched. Despite this negative comment, those investors later included both the Duke of Wellington and Thomas Telford, the great British canal-builder.*   Keefer, p. 14

Even in 1818, when Merritt had made his first rough survey for a possible route, the idea of a canal across the Niagara Peninsula had not been new, and in fact several different routes had already been suggested. The Niagara Escarpment was a formidable hindrance to navigation between lakes Erie and Ontario, since the natural line of drainage along the Niagara River was beset by a triple hazard in the form of the rapids, the falls and the narrow gorge of the middle length of the river. These obstructions had been offset by portage roads to link the upper and lower stretches of the river, first on the American bank and later (after American Independence in 1783) on the British side. Even so, costs and delays of unloading goods, hauling them by wagon across the steep slope of the Escarpment, reloading them onto river boats, and then transferring them to lake schooners inhibited trade and could only prove prohibitory once the easier route along the Erie Canal became accessible. In addition, the portage route was dangerously close to the American border and, given the booming economy and aggressive foreign policy of the United States at that time, a safer route, further inland, seemed vital to the survival of Upper Canada.

Furthermore, another aspect which could scarcely have escaped the notice of men with business concerns in the fledgling communities of the Niagara Peninsula was the potential of a canal to attract population to its environs [Fig. 13]. Ports at strategic intervals, canal-side service settlements (first during construction, then for maintenance of the canal, for both men and draft animals), and the settlement of land in the area would all accompany the increase of goods which could move at a lower cost year by year. Then, too, the waters of a canal, through which goods-laden ships pass, would also provide power for industrial development, which in its turn would act as a magnet for urban growth [Fig. 14].

1.13 **The Farmers' Journal and Welland Canal Intelligencer:** *The masthead of Merritt's newspaper (the first in St. Catharines), inaugurated in 1826 to promote the canal, shows wharves and warehouses, a steamer and a schooner, barrels, bales and boxes — all symbolizing the prosperity which the Welland Canal Company believed the waterway would bring, not only to the canal-side communities, but to the province as a whole.*
The Farmers' Journal..., 1826

1.14 Canal-Based Prosperity at Lockport, N.Y., 1881: *Visiting Lockport on 19 July 1823 Merritt recorded in his journal that the town "bids fair to become a large and flourishing city."*[16] *He and his colleagues hoped that Niagara towns would grow and flourish, thanks to a canal on Canadian soil.*   Harper's, p. 429

Merritt and his friends could not have foreseen the scale and scope of the St. Lawrence Seaway, the extent and complexity of urban development, and the process of almost continuous re-creation of the landscape of the Niagara Peninsula, which resulted from the evolution of their canal [Fig. 15]. But Merritt at least had the prescience, at the sod-turning ceremony in 1824 [Fig. 16], to predict that, when the canal was finished, "Instead of remaining in this dull, supine state, in which we have been for years past, we will mingle in the bustle and active scenes of business...."[17]

Despite this visionary statement, Merritt was essentially a man of business. In early 1825 he wrote to his father-in-law, "my whole personal interest in this undertaking is the value it will attach to my property on the route...."[18]

The combination of vision and self-interest was to produce an economic revolution, as H.G.J. Aitken, a 20th-century historian, wrote:

Precisely when and by whom the possibilities which lay behind Merritt's crude and amateurish survey [of 18 September 1818] were first realized is a matter for conjecture.... By the fourteenth of October, when the survey and plans were presented at a public meeting in Niagara, the project had already grown beyond its original bounds. From a ditch to convey water, it had become a canal to carry boats.[19]

The rest is history [Fig. 17].

1.15 Four Canals at the Escarpment, ca. 1928: *Merritt's scheme began a process of massive earth-moving and water-channeling which, if not exactly "uninterrupted," has certainly continued at intervals ever since. Here, between Merritton and Thorold, the First Canal (lower centre) and the Second Canal (lower right) "climb the mountain." The Third Canal curves in a wide arc across the top of the picture, while the Fourth is under construction in the middle distance (with two pairs of the flight locks visible).*
St. Catharines Centennial Library

1.16 Allanburg, 30 November 1979: *On the 150th anniversary of the Welland Canal opening, a descendant of George Keefer (left) and actor David Mackenzie (playing Merritt) re-enacted the original sod-turning at Allanburg. As Keefer took the spade on 30 November 1824, he said: "Gentlemen, it is with pleasure that I remove the first earth from the Welland Canal, and ardently hope the work may continue uninterrupted until the whole is completed."*[20]   Arden Phair

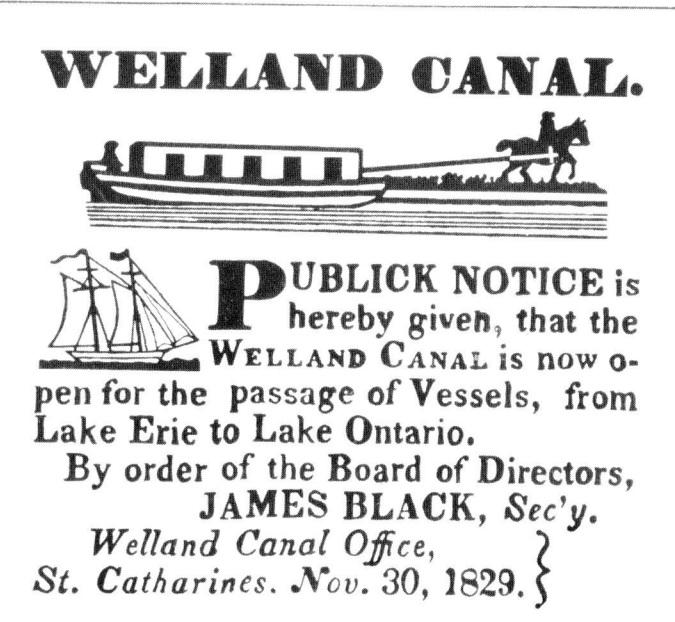

1.17 St. Johns Outdoor Studies Centre

2.1 The Niagara Escarpment, 1904: *The most obvious of the many obstacles to water communication between lakes Erie and Ontario was overcome by a series of locks, which carried both the First and Second Canals "up the mountain" on nearly the same site. "Neptune's Staircase" is still to be seen in Mountain Locks Park in St. Catharines. The photograph, showing hand-operated gears above the sluices (or valves) in the gates, was taken when this stretch of the Second Canal no longer carried vessels, but still provided water power for several mills in the area.* AO: ST-406

2. OVERCOMING THE PHYSICAL PROBLEMS

The most obvious physical problem, and one for which the solution provides the most striking landmarks, was the Niagara Escarpment [Fig. 1], rising some 184 feet (56 m). Cataracts such as DeCew Falls, which provided a head of water for turning mill wheels, are picturesque indeed [see Chap. 1, Fig. 5]: nevertheless the height of the Escarpment was one of the major obstacles to navigation of the Niagara River, with its spectacular but obstructive falls linking lakes Erie and Ontario.

The original idea for Merritt's canal was for it to "climb the mountain" by means of an incline railway — a solution which was well known in British canal construction [Fig. 2]. Vague knowledge of an 18th-century incline (thought to have been built by the French) was common in the Niagara Peninsula in the 19th century. That incline had served to haul up bateaux and supplies from the Niagara River near Lewiston, N.Y. Where the actual plan to use such a device for the Welland came from, we do not know.

In any event, the planners realized from the beginning that locks might have to be employed instead, and in fact an incline soon became impracticable. Original plans allowed for the passage of bateaux and barges only, but investors in New York City urged that the canal dimensions be enlarged to accommodate larger vessels, even steamers. Once this decision had been reached, the point at issue became the exact route which should be followed by the canal.

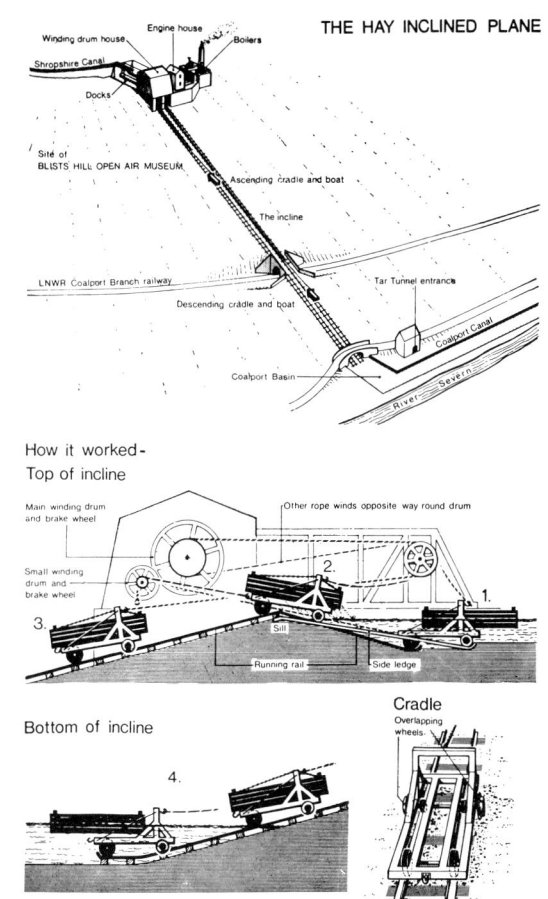

2.2 Coalport, England: *Built ca. 1793-94, the Hay Inclined Plane, or incline railway, was but one of many on British canals. It may have inspired the original plan for getting ships over the Niagara Escarpment. Such inclines were capable of lifting only small boats or barges similar in tonnage to the boats and bateaux proposed for the original Erie and Welland canals.*
Ironbridge Gorge Museum Trust

This became a contentious matter and, in fact, the route of the original canal underwent a number of alterations [see Chap. 1, Fig. 9]. For all early canal builders, a guiding principle in choosing a route was to utilize existing waterways and to follow the contours of the land, whenever possible, to reduce the number and size of locks required. (Of course the location of mills, and the urgings or objections from local residents had to be considered as well.) Hence the route of the first two canals, and to a certain extent the third, followed natural contours, especially in climbing the Escarpment [Fig. 1].

Although masonry locks were being built in Britain, on the Continent, in the United States – and even for the military canals in Lower Canada – the difficulty in raising sufficient funds resulted in the construction of the much cheaper wooden locks for the Welland. It proved a false economy, with constant repairs leading to frequent holdups for canal trade. So it was not surprising that, when the government of Upper Canada took over the running of the Welland Canal in 1842 (following the Act of Union of 1841), a thorough reconstruction of the canal was undertaken (1842-45) as part of a concerted effort to improve the whole St. Lawrence waterway, to link the Atlantic with the Great Lakes [Fig. 1].

When the Welland was rebuilt again in the later 19th century, a new and more direct route was chosen, and another set of impressive stone locks was added to the landscape [Fig. 3]. Hardly was the Third Canal (1874-87) completed before it, too, required enlargement, with another change of route and a new construction material (reinforced concrete) being employed. With each reconstruction, the size of the locks increased and their number decreased [Figs. 4, 5].

2.3 Near St. Catharines, 1980: *A "gold mine" for industrial archaeologists, the sturdy cut stone walls of the flight locks of the Third Canal still carry overflow from the present waterway in a parklike area south of Glendale Avenue. The gradual approach taken here, mounting the side of the Escarpment, was typical of early canal building.*   R.R. Taylor

2.4 Thorold, ca. 1925: *By the 1920s current technology permitted a "head-on" attack on the Escarpment, as opposed to the lengthier approach taken earlier. Blasting and excavating down through the limestone, workers then built upwards with massive walls of concrete, creating in the process a breathtaking man-made landscape, soon to be engulfed in water. Here we see the breast-wall excavation at the head of the twinned Lock 4. (See Frontispiece for a spectacular view of the Flight Locks of the Fourth Canal.)* Cowan, p. 42

2.5 Port Weller, 1928: *The huge gates at Lock 1 are ready for service. Kept in constant good repair, these gates are still in operation. Water enters or leaves the lock through valves at either end. Earlier canals had the water passing through sluices in the gates (First and Second Canals), or walls (Third Canal).* PAC: PA-43517

A less spectacular but even greater problem than the massive lift at the Escarpment was that of obtaining an adequate water supply. The original idea had been to use the Welland River, but this required too deep a cut between Allanburg and Port Robinson. Problems were encountered, and an alternative had to be found. Using Lake Erie would have required an even deeper cut, so ultimately the Grand River, flowing into Lake Erie, was utilized by means of a "feeder" canal cutting across a marshy area to join the Welland Canal at what became the town of Welland. Opened in 1829, it was driven 27 miles (43 km) through the Cranberry Marsh, from Dunnville to Port Robinson [Fig. 6]. The Grand River was dammed almost four miles (6 km) from its mouth on Lake Erie, and the Feeder continued to provide a regular supply of water to the canal until 1887, in the process passing over the Welland River by means of a wooden aqueduct (hence the original name of Welland – "Aqueduct"!).

2.6 The Feeder Canal, 1979: *The skill of the early surveyors is apparent in the line of the Feeder, which still stretches straight across the rural countryside.*　　J.N. Jackson

2.7 Welland, 1882: *The Second Canal aqueduct, with the still surviving County Court House in the background. Steam power had obviously "arrived" and in the foreground (reflecting ever-changing technology) construction proceeds with another newer (and larger) aqueduct required for the Third Canal.*　　Picturesque Canada, 1882

Flimsy but effective, that first aqueduct, 365 feet (111 m) long, 24 feet (7 m) wide, and about five feet (1.5 m) deep, with walkways on both sides, carried the Feeder from 1829 to 1842, when it was rebuilt in stone [Fig. 7]. After 1887 Lake Erie replaced the Grand River as a source of water supply [Fig. 8], but an aqueduct remained at Welland, a new stone one, to carry the Third Canal over the river [Fig. 9]. By the 1920s successive aqueducts had carried vessels of ever-increasing size over the Welland River for over a hundred years. But by then, such a deep channel was required to accommodate the ships that a new solution had to be found: the answer was a concrete syphon culvert [Fig. 10].

2.8 Port Colborne, ca. 1885: *This photograph, reminiscent of a Roman bath, shows a conduit under construction just north of the present bridges. Although the site is now covered with buildings, it is still intact underground. The Grand Trunk Railway grain elevator, built in 1858, is in the distance.* William Koudys Coll.

2.9 Welland, ca. 1910: *"The most stupendous piece of masonwork to be found in Upper Canada," an anonymous visitor noted of the Third Canal aqueduct in 1887. A freighter makes a smooth passage over the Welland River, with the Alexandra swing bridge (1901) open in the background. The Riverside Mill is on the left; the lock in the foreground carried canal traffic to the river.*
Francis Petrie Coll.

2.10 Welland, ca. 1937: *The syphon culvert devised to carry the river under the canal in six concrete underground tubes. The Fourth Canal concrete structure may be less picturesque than cut stone arches, but it is no less functional.*   John Burtniak Coll.

2.11 The Deep Cut, 1882: *When the tunnel planned to carry the canal through the low ridge between Allanburg and Port Robinson had to be abandoned in 1827, an artificial valley was created. Men used picks, shovels and scrapers, with the help of Phelps' machine [see Chap. 3, Fig. 4]. This view indicates the depth to which cutting was required.*   Picturesque Canada, 1882

The builders of the original canal had faced another problem, one closely related to that of water supply: getting through another, lesser height of land, just south of the Niagara Escarpment. Once again the original idea, to use a tunnel (the preferred solution in Britain), had to be abandoned when water seepage caused landslides and made tunnelling impossible. Instead, an open cut (the "Deep Cut") was made, using unskilled labour and the most primitive methods [Fig. 11]. Even the Third Canal improvements were accomplished mainly by human and animal labour — although by the time construction began on the Fourth Canal in 1913, steam shovels were being employed [Fig. 12], but not exclusively [see Chap. 6, Fig. 8].

2.12 The Deep Cut, 1914: *Despite considerable advances in technology since the 1820s, the first clearing for the Fourth Canal still required considerable animal power to draw the "stoneboats." More advanced technically, the mobile crane moves on temporary tracks: an example of contemporary equipment undergoing constant change and development (for other cranes, see Chap. 3).* PAC: PA-61103

Merely procuring an adequate supply of water did not end the water problem: it had to be "managed." Mention has been made of the aqueduct used to carry the Feeder over the Welland River, and this conflict between natural and created waterway had to be tackled with each successive rebuilding. So too did the problem of controlling the level of water at the Lake Erie end of the canal — resolved by building "control" locks at Port Colborne [Fig. 13]. In addition, the natural force of seasonal changes, not to mention stormy weather, required the construction of protective breakwaters at both ends of the canal [Fig. 14; and see Chap. 10, Figs. 5, 8]. Even then, further measures to control the flow and supply of water along the canal, particularly in the vicinity of the locks, were required: hence the raceways, and numerous weirs and ponds [Figs. 15, 18; and see Fig. 1].

2.13 Port Colborne, ca. 1887: *The twin control locks, with East Street (demolished for Fourth Canal construction) and the Grand Trunk Railway elevator. Chain winches are used to pull open the lock gates, replacing the earlier "balance beams" (see Chap. 3, Fig. 5).* William Koudys Coll.

2.14 Port Weller, 1914: *Dredges, tugs, scows and steam locomotives bring tons of earth and rock to fill concrete cribs sunk into Lake Ontario, to create the piers for the Fourth Canal. Despite the massiveness of the structure, much of it was smashed by winter storms during the period when construction was halted by World War I.* SCHM: N-1340

2.15 St. Catharines, ca. 1871: *An obvious location for water-powered mills was near the locks, but this limited the number of mills and factories, and the expanding economy could not be accommodated. Construction of raceways allowed other sites to be utilized. In fact, anywhere that the water could be passed over a mill wheel became a suitable location for a factory. The raceway here forked into two terraced channels, allowing construction of many more mills.* DeVolpi (*Can. Illust. News*, 1871)

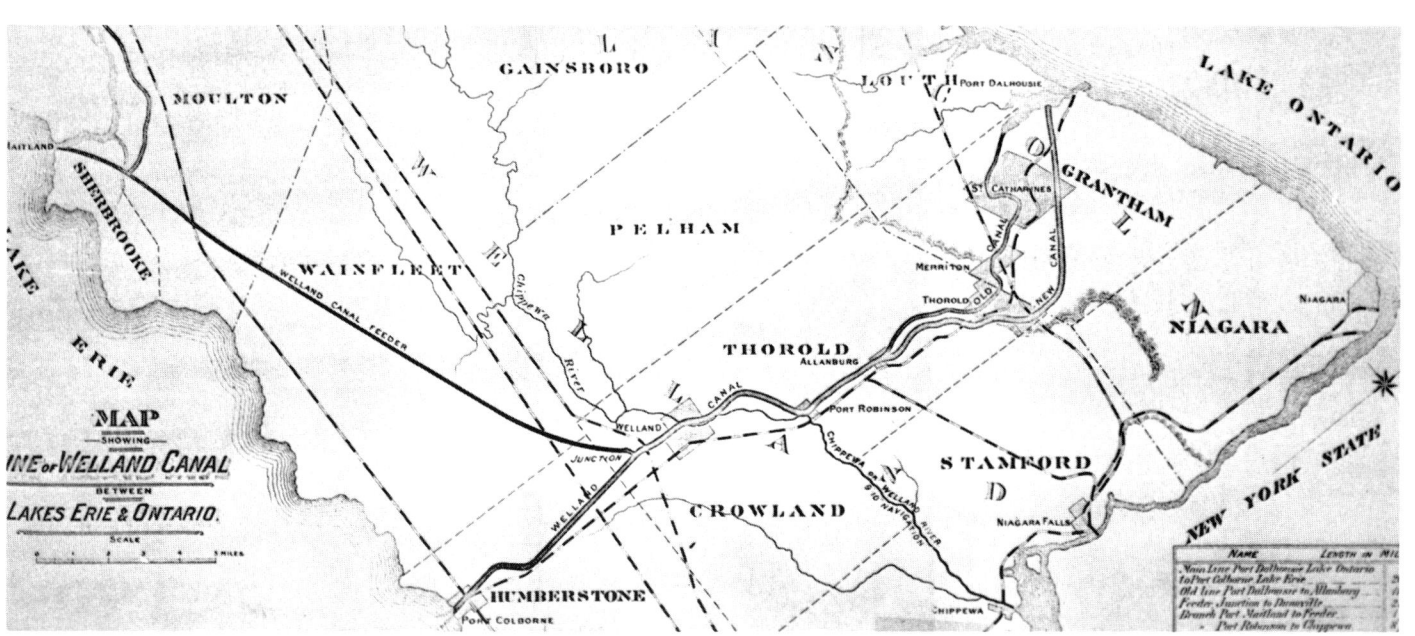

2.16 "The Great Welland Canal," 1895: *A map produced by the Department of Railways and Canals records the changes wrought over nearly 75 years (see Chap. 1, Fig. 8), as the Niagara Peninsula was about to enter the 20th century. The canal communities had enjoyed spectacular growth, stimulated by the canal and the nearly parallel Welland Railway (opened 1859).* Dept. of Railways and Canals, Annual Report 1894-95

Of two other problems which pertained chiefly to the First Canal, only one was in itself physical: the marshy land through which the extension to Lake Erie, and the Feeder, had to be built. The agues and fevers associated with the area would, it was hoped, be lessened once the Feeder began to drain the area. But during construction various ills, including "malaria," were commonplace. The second of the difficulties which pertained chiefly to the First Canal was that of obtaining adequate financing [see Introduction, p. xvi] – every bit as crucial as acquiring adequate water supplies.

While some problems were ongoing, and that of the marsh was confined mainly to the First Canal, a new difficulty was encountered by the builders of the Third Canal. By 1874, when the Third Canal was begun, the "Railway Age" had arrived, ushering in a major and continuing problem: the conflict between surface and water traffic [Fig. 16]. Needless to say, passage of ships proved disruptive to surface traffic, but the only alternative to bridges was tunnelling [Fig. 17], and this was not always practicable, given the routes and technology of the times [see Chap. 10], hence the "swing" bridges so characteristic of the Third Canal, and the later, but even more noticeable, "lift" bridges of the Fourth [Fig. 18; and see Chap. 7, Figs. 13, 16, 24; Chap. 10, Fig. 21].

2.17 Near Thorold, ca. 1885: *The conflict between canal and railways was usually resolved by carrying the latter over the canal by bridges (see Chap. 10, Fig. 15), but in the case of the Grank Trunk Railway the solution was a tunnel. It was created by excavating a cutting for the trailway tracks, lining it with stone, then covering it with stone vaults and finally with earth. Then the canal channel was built – above the railway. Nearby, St. David's Road was taken under the Third Canal by the same means.*   William Koudys Coll.

2.18 Near Lock Three, 1920s: *During construction of the Fourth Canal, navigation had to continue along the Third Canal (cutting diagonally across the picture), with its large weir ponds and typical swing bridge (centre right). This exacerbated difficulties caused by landslides, which slowed the building of Lock 3 (foreground). Between Lock 3 and the new twin flight locks at Thorold (rising in the background) a lift bridge can be seen. Workers and engineers of the first three Welland Canals would have sympathized with their counterparts in the 1920s, for they had all faced the dangers posed by handling large volumes of water.*
PAC: PA-43944

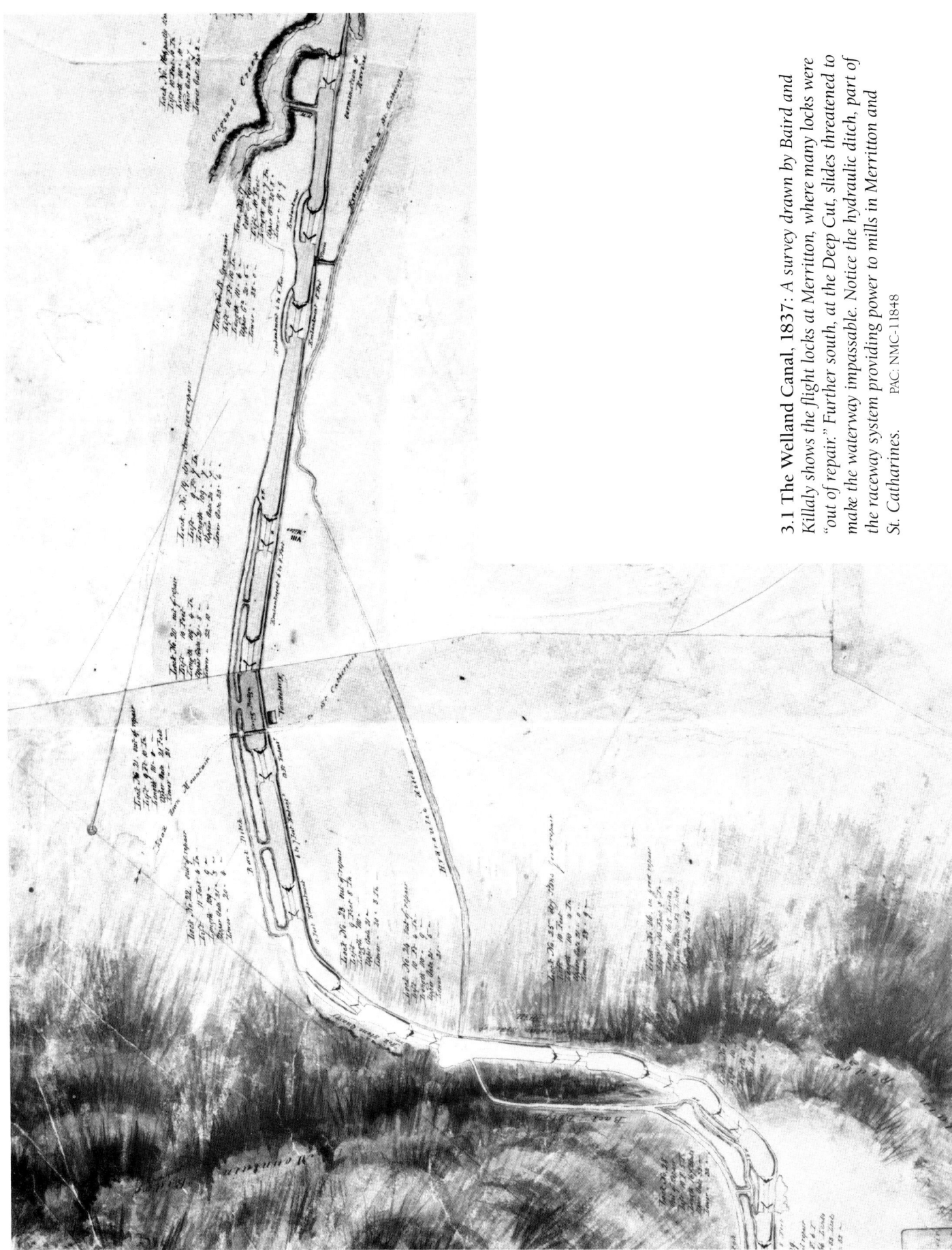

3.1 The Welland Canal, 1837: A survey drawn by Baird and Killaly shows the flight locks at Merritton, where many locks were "out of repair." Further south, at the Deep Cut, slides threatened to make the waterway impassable. Notice the hydraulic ditch, part of the raceway system providing power to mills in Merritton and St. Catharines.   PAC: NMC-11848

3. MEN WITH MACHINES

People often say that men with ideas respond to changes wrought by technology, but we sometimes forget that they are at the same time constrained by the technology available to them. Nowhere is this more evident than in the history of the Welland Canals. Changes in shipbuilding technology [Fig. 2] – in the size as well as numbers of ships built – were (as they still are) the "great imperatives" dictating periodic reconstructions of, and alterations to, the Welland [see Chap. 1, Fig.1]. An additional factor in the late 1830s was the state of disrepair into which the original canal, with its wooden locks and iron hardware, had fallen, and in 1837 two British engineers, Hamilton Killaly and N. H. Baird, were hired to survey the canal route and recommend changes and improvements [Fig. 1].

The building of the original canal was accomplished largely through the efforts of men using picks and shovels, scrapers, and barrows and carts drawn by horses and mules – primitive technology indeed! But even such limited equipment was not available in the Upper Canada of the mid-1820s [Fig. 3]. When William Hamilton Merritt was questioned by a Select Committee of the Legislature on 30 November 1825 regarding a petition for remission of import duties, he stated: "The proper Spades and Shovels are not imported here [i.e., to Upper Canada from Britain], but are made in the United-States." Further inquiry led him to say: "Waggons could not be procured in this country at a reasonable price, or in sufficient quantity."[21]

While this may seem surprising, it should be noted that even the builders of the Erie Canal, from 1817 on, had to *teach themselves* how to build their own machinery to do such things as break up matted turf, move earth and rock, cut roots and pull stumps. It was some of the contractors who had learned on-the-job on the Erie who brought their horses, oxen and equipment to work on the Welland.

3.2 St. Catharines, ca. 1862: *The canaller on the right awaits passage through Lock 3 of the Second Canal, opposite the Lincoln and Welland sawmill run by Thomas Rodman Merritt (a son of the canal-builder). Such vessels, built with boxlike hulls to fit canal locks, were derived from traditional schooners, which had flared bows and wide transoms. Their increasing size had made the First Canal obsolete, and by this time were already putting pressure on the Second Canal.*   St. Johns Outdoor Studies Centre

For example, when in 1827 the directors of the Welland Canal Company advertised for designs for an earth-moving machine, it was the American contractor Oliver Phelps who devised the first "machine" to be used on the Welland [Fig. 4]. His ingenious scheme for moving earth in the Deep Cut excavations somewhat eased the lot of both men and animals. Phelps had come to the Niagara area as a sub-contractor with Messrs. Hovey and Beach, the original contractors for the Deep Cut (also Americans). The problems they had encountered drove them to bankruptcy by September 1827, and Phelps took over the work.

The problems regarding locks — size and material — have already been mentioned (Chap. 2). In essence, a lock is simply a chamber (in the early days it was usually made of stone or brick) with watertight gates at either end and sluices which regulate the level of water inside [Fig. 5]. A vessel entering an empty lock can be raised when the lock has been filled; one entering a full lock will be lowered as the lock is emptied. Pioneering canal-builders in Massachusetts had been advised (in 1794) by a visiting Englishman who had worked with Brindley that wood (which was plentiful) was not as good as stone for the lock walls. The only slightly more experienced, and equally self-taught, men who designed the Erie Canal in New York State "had to find out that wood was not a sensible material for locks."[22]

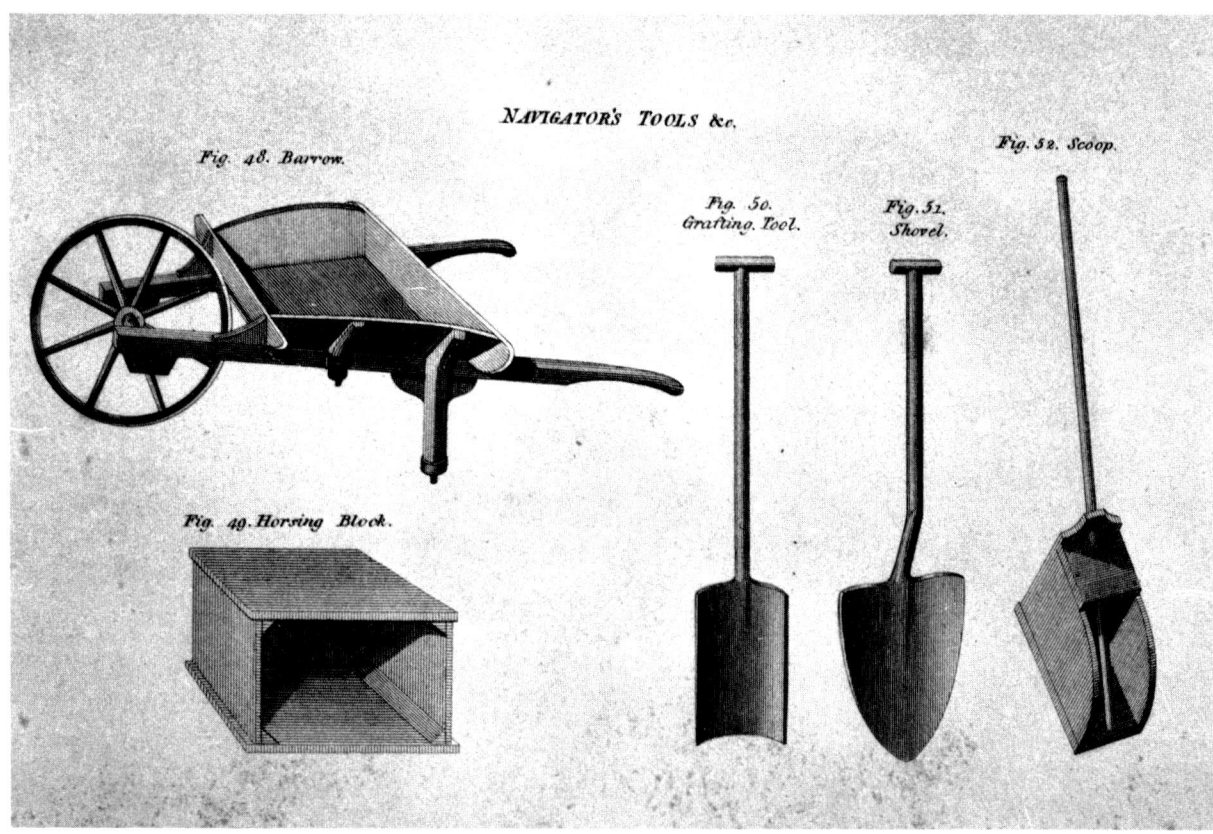

3.3 A Navvy's Simple Tools, ca. 1820: *Abraham Rees' Cyclopedia, known to Merritt and others in the Niagara Peninsula, devoted much space to canal-building in England and the U.S.A., including carefully rendered drawings of the latest refinements in shovels, scoops, and barrows. But what was a "horsing block"? [See also Chap. 6, Fig. 3]*   Rees, Vol. II, plate vii

3.5 Near Audlem, England, 1985 (opposite, bottom): *Two teenagers pull on the balance beam to open the top gate of a lock on the Shropshire Union Canal — still a familiar scene on most British canals. The lock gates of early canals in North America (including the Welland) were operated in similar fashion, with locktenders responsible for the hand-operation of the gates.*   R.M. Styran

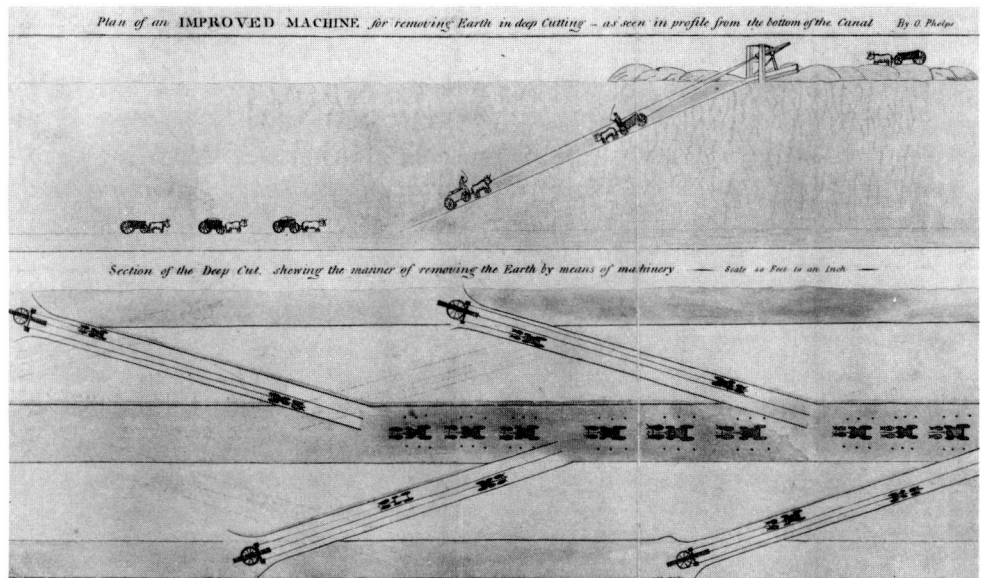

3.4 Oliver Phelps' Earth-Moving Machine, ca. 1827: *Phelps' machine fixed a wagon wheel to the top of a seven-foot (2.1 m) post at the top of the canal bank; then a rope with a hook on each end was fixed around the wheel, extending to the bottom of the channel. One hook was attached to a cart going down, and the other to an already loaded cart below. The descending cart, and gravity, helped to pull the loaded cart up to the top. Phelps (1779-1851) settled in the area and founded a dynasty of mill-owners in Merritton. As described by a contemporary:*

Mr. Phelps was not one of those old fussey fogies or dandy doolittle contractors of whom you read ... and who accomplished next to nothing, but was a hard working, active, stirring and wide-awake driving person, who always said to his laborers, come boys, follow me, instead of go men and do this and that, as is too often the case; but wherever there was any hard work, heavy lifting, mud, water, slush or dirt in the way, he always bounced in first and foremost and lead the way.[24]   PAC: C-101265; Tuer, p. 1

45

Nevertheless, on 4 July 1825 the Welland Canal Company offered a one hundred dollar "premium" for "the best Model of a Wooden Lock, or Stone and wood connected…. The object of the Board is to obtain the most perfect plan to combine solidity and duration and be constructed on *the most simple and cheapest method*" [emphasis added][23]. This despite the contrary advice from one of the Erie's "engineers," consulted in 1824. By 1825, too, the original plan for the canal, which had called for a nine-foot (2.7 m) wide tunnel, and eight-foot (2.4 m) wide locks, had been discarded. The Company Report dated 1 February 1825 notes: "The propriety of enlarging it to fifteen feet [ca. 4.5 m] wide, fourteen feet [ca. 4.3 m] high and eight feet [2.4 m] water [i.e., depth], the size of the Erie Canal, was suggested to us and has been adopted."[25] After considerable debate, the lock size was finally settled at 110 feet by 22 feet (33.5 x 6.7 m), but the choice of wood as the construction material remained [Fig. 6].

3.6 St. Catharines, 1987: *Successive reconstructions have destroyed or buried the First Canal locks. Today, only two are known to survive. Excavation of Lock 24 of the First Canal, in the summer of 1987, provided a wealth of information for canal and engineering historians and drew hundreds of spectators of all ages. Here a school group watches as excavators near maximum depth, exposing almost complete remains of the lock gates. The iron hardware has been removed to the St. Catharines Historical Museum. The lock has had to be re-buried in order to preserve the wood.*
Welland Canals Society

3.7 The Coming of Steam: *The steamship VANDALIA, built 1841 at Oswego, N.Y., seen in the Second Canal, exemplifies the growing size and power of ships which the Welland had to accommodate in order to survive. She was the first to have machinery installed aft, and the first steam propeller to be built for commercial purposes.* Cuthbertson, p. 221

By the 1840s, when the canal was reconstructed for the first time, the Upper Canada government financed not merely the enlargement required to accommodate the larger vessels, including steamers [Fig. 7], but also the use of the more durable limestone [Fig. 8]. Smooth-faced blocks were shaped by hand specifically to fulfill the requirements of lock walls: smooth, not to damage wooden hulls; curved wall ends to act as buffers; and recessed sections for the lock gates. Both walls slant slightly, making the channel wider at the top than at the bottom, to provide a cushion of water to protect passing ships.

3.8 Lasting Craftsmanship: *"New and magnificent, and substantial locks . . . . the [stone]work of which is equal to that of any public work in the world…," exclaimed W.H. Smith in his Gazetteer in 1846.[26] The surveyors had suggested using local limestone for the locks, as it would be more durable in view of the wash from the steam-powered vessels then using the canal. In the 1840s most of the builders' supplies, such as the lock gate hinges, had to come by water from Québec – and these endured for over a century. The lock walls at the Escarpment have also outlasted the steamships!* Arden Phair

3.9 Near Woking, England, ca. 1912: *This repair scene on the Basingstoke Canal typifies not only the working conditions and equipment of the first two Welland Canals, but also demonstrates the kind of wooden lock gates used on the First Canal. Note the balance beams which were operated by hand in the early days of the Welland, as they still are on many canals in Britain to this day [see Fig. 5].* Moorland Publishing Company

Nevertheless, and despite the use of steam engines in ships, the Second Canal was built largely by the traditional methods – men with picks, shovels and scrapers, with materials transported by animal-drawn carts [Fig. 9]. Under such conditions, the canal contractors were the key men, acting under the general direction of government engineers [Fig. 10].

3.10 John Brown, Contractor (inset): *An immigrant Scottish stonecutter, one of many attracted to the canal works, Brown became a stone contractor for both the Second Canal and the Welland Railway. Later his company assisted in the construction of the Third Canal. His portrait exemplifies the pride and rectitude of the 19th century "self-made man."*   Page's Atlas

3.11 At the Escarpment, 1874-1887: *Mules used to draw specially devised carts with low-slung carriages (stone-boats), minimized the lifting of the heavy slabs of limestone (a later version of this sort of cart may be seen at the Port Colborne Historical and Marine Museum). Hand-operated winches operated the cranes.*
William Koudys Coll.

3.12 Steam Power in Construction, 1874-1887: *While human and animal power were still very much in evidence during construction of the Third Canal, the operators and their families proudly show off the "very latest" in modern equipment, a steam-powered shovel.*   William Koudys Coll.

Even the Third Canal (1874-1887) still relied heavily on the traditional methods, although by then the "stone-boat" (a special type of low-slung cart) had been devised to facilitate the handling of heavy blocks of limestone [Fig. 11]. Technology derived from the burgeoning railways was adapted to canal construction; steam engines and shovels were utilized [Fig. 12], as well as mobile cranes moving on tracks [Figs. 13, 14].

3.13 More Machinery, 1874-1887: *Mobile scaffolds, made of wood and running on tracks set into the lock walls, supported four cranes used to lift and place the great limestone blocks.*   SCHM: L967.112.5

3.14 Welland, ca. 1880: *Another type of mobile crane looms in the upper right, crossing the arches of what was to be the third — and last — aqueduct at Welland (277 feet long, 85 feet wide, 16 feet deep; 84 by 26 by 5 m). In 1928 this solidly built structure was demolished, and the contractor complained that its destruction took much longer than planned and cost more than anticipated: such was the skill of 19th-century stonemasons. The equally durable Second Canal aqueduct beside it was kept in service and survives still.*   SCHM: N-4618

The Welland and the Grand Trunk Railways, as well as the Second Canal, were used to bring stone, timber, cement and other heavy material to the building sites [Fig. 15]. Improvements in steel-making resulted in the older forms of iron being superseded, although not entirely. In addition to the new methods, a new route was chosen, with a further reduction of the number of locks required. So for the first time since the canal first carried vessels, it no longer carried them through the heart of St. Catharines [see Chap. 1, Fig. 1].

3.15 At the Escarpment, 1874-1887: *While steam engines were being used, horses and mules still pulled loaded carts on temporary wooden rails in the deepening channels and locks of the Third Canal.*   SCHM: N-1005

The technological advances resulted in another change: the appearance of the professional "civil engineer" as the person responsible for the overall construction of such major projects as the Third Welland Canal. It is perhaps fitting that Thomas Coltrin Keefer (twelfth son of Merritt's friend and co-promoter of the original canal, George Keefer) became known as the "Dean of Canadian Engineers" [Fig. 16]. The Keefer residence had been "home" for many of the canal's pioneering engineers, and young Thomas grew up hearing about the challenges they faced and their search for solutions.

So rapid was the pace of technological development in the latter half of the 19th century, that a Royal Commission appointed to examine Inland Navigation in Canada reported, in 1871: "The tendency in ship-building for the last quarter of a century on the Upper Lakes has been to construct larger vessels every way whether propelled by steam or sails; while the screw is superseding the paddle everywhere, on the Lakes as well as on the ocean, the relative number and tonnage of screw steamers is gradually increasing upon the sailing craft."[27]

As a result of their inquiry, the Commission recommended a uniform size for all locks of the St. Lawrence and Welland Canals, and the proposed canal at Sault Ste. Marie: 270 feet by 45 feet, with 12 feet of draught over the sills (82.3 m by 13.7 m by 3.7 m), with the canals to be 100 feet (30.5 m) in width, to allow two vessels to pass. Despite this enlargement, by the end of the 19th century, with the Third Canal only recently completed, the still-increasing size (and number) of ships necessitated yet another rebuilding [Fig. 17] and another route change, along with even further reduction in the number of locks required (especially at the Escarpment). This time a new building material was available: concrete, reinforced with steel rods [Fig. 18]. Even so, the massive steel gates now possible [see Chap. 2, Fig. 5] required further technological developments in order to handle them efficiently, and safely.

3.16 Thomas Coltrin Keefer (1821-1915), ca. 1863: *As a divisional engineer in his youth he helped to plan the Second Canal, experience which led to work on the Ottawa and St. Lawrence Canals. He was the first president of the Canadian Society of Civil Engineers. Described as "one of the most effective propagandists in the nineteenth century for the vital economic significance of the St. Lawrence – Great Lakes Commercial System," he felt it was "created by God to ensure the greatest good to the greatest number of inhabitants of North America."*[28]   Can. Illust. News, Sept. 26, 1863

Building the Fourth Canal took over 20 years, as the First World War, labour troubles and economic problems intervened. Surveys had begun in 1908 and actual construction in 1913. But since it was believed that the war which broke out in 1914 would be short, work on the canal was not halted until 1917, when the pressures on men and materials became acute in the face of the possibility of defeat. In the early stages of construction, before the First World War intervened, men and their mule- or horse-drawn carts were still a common sight in the construction areas [Fig. 19; see Chap. 6, Fig. 8].

3.17 Port Dalhousie, 1928: *This crowded scene illustrates the need for yet another rebuilding of the Welland Canal.*   SCHM: N-1441

3.18 Lock Two, St. Catharines, ca. 1960: *By mid-20th century, concrete had replaced cut limestone, steel ships were the rule, and technological change continued, as steam power gave way to diesel fuel. The size of ships grows ever larger and already poses (again) the question which has led to constant rebuilding: when, how, and at what cost will a new canal be built?*   SCHM: N-4302

3.19 Pre-World War I Construction: *A 1913 scene recalls construction of the Third Canal, just 35 years earlier. The cars were specially built for use on the waterway.*   PAC: PA-61137

By the time work resumed in 1919, however, the animal-powered carts were increasingly being replaced by sophisticated machinery — now powered by steam engines, of course [Fig. 20]. By the time construction was completed in 1932, there could be no doubt as to the need for the enlarged waterway [Fig. 21]. The formal opening, which took place at the flight locks in Thorold, was celebrated with great pomp and attended by dignitaries from as far away as India [Fig. 22]. The crucial role of the engineers and their trusted supervisors was recognized and earned them, too, a place at the ceremonies [Fig. 23].

3.20 Thorold, ca. 1929: *By the later 1920s, when construction resumed, remarkably "modern"-looking equipment was available. This steel concreting tower was about 150 feet (46 m) high, and ran on 12 wheels set on a 33-foot (10 m) gauge track. More sophisticated than its predecessor of 50 years before [see Figs. 13, 14], it was another example of the technological progress served and stimulated by the needs of canal-building.*
Cowan, p. 34

3.21 Port Weller, 1931: *Lakers and salties await entrance to Lock 1 of the new canal which, although not formally opened until 1932, was obviously urgently needed. The northern terminus was named after John Laing Weller, who had been born in Cobourg, Ontario, and had worked on the Trent-Severn and St. Lawrence Canals before becoming superintendent of the Welland in 1900. In 1912 he was put in charge of all construction for the Fourth Canal.*   Canada. Dept. of Railways and Canals

3.22 Thorold, 8 August 1932: *The Governor General, the Earl of Bessborough, moves a lever to raise the fender at the upper end of Lock 6: the official "opening" (top centre). Top right, Chief Engineer Alexander J. Grant with his family; centre right, Stanley Baldwin and J.H. Thomas, British delegates to the British Empire Economic Conference; lower right, the Governor General reviews the guard of honour; lower left, the Governor General greets Grant; top left, the Governor General with the Begum, wife of Haji Abdullah Haroon of India and their daughter. Truly an international occasion!*   St. Catharines Centennial Library

3.23 Thorold, 8 August 1932: *Less exalted, but equally deserving of a place in posterity, the engineers (some with their wives) pose between two of the twinned flight locks, with numerous supervisors crowding the stairway. Alexander Grant, appropriately, is seated in the centre front (between two ladies in cloche hats). Grant, an irascible Scot, "had a policy of bawling somebody out every day," recalls a contemporary, but he effectively supervised the completion of an engineering masterpiece.* Welland Historical Museum

Throughout its history, then, the Welland Canal has reflected both the benefits and the challenges of advances in technology. Today its operating centres resemble "space age" control rooms, utilizing the most sophisticated electronic systems [see Chap. 6, Fig. 21]. William Hamilton Merritt might well be astounded by the nature and profusion of the equipment; he would certainly beam with delight at the ways in which his vision has continued to respond to the needs – and capabilities – of society.

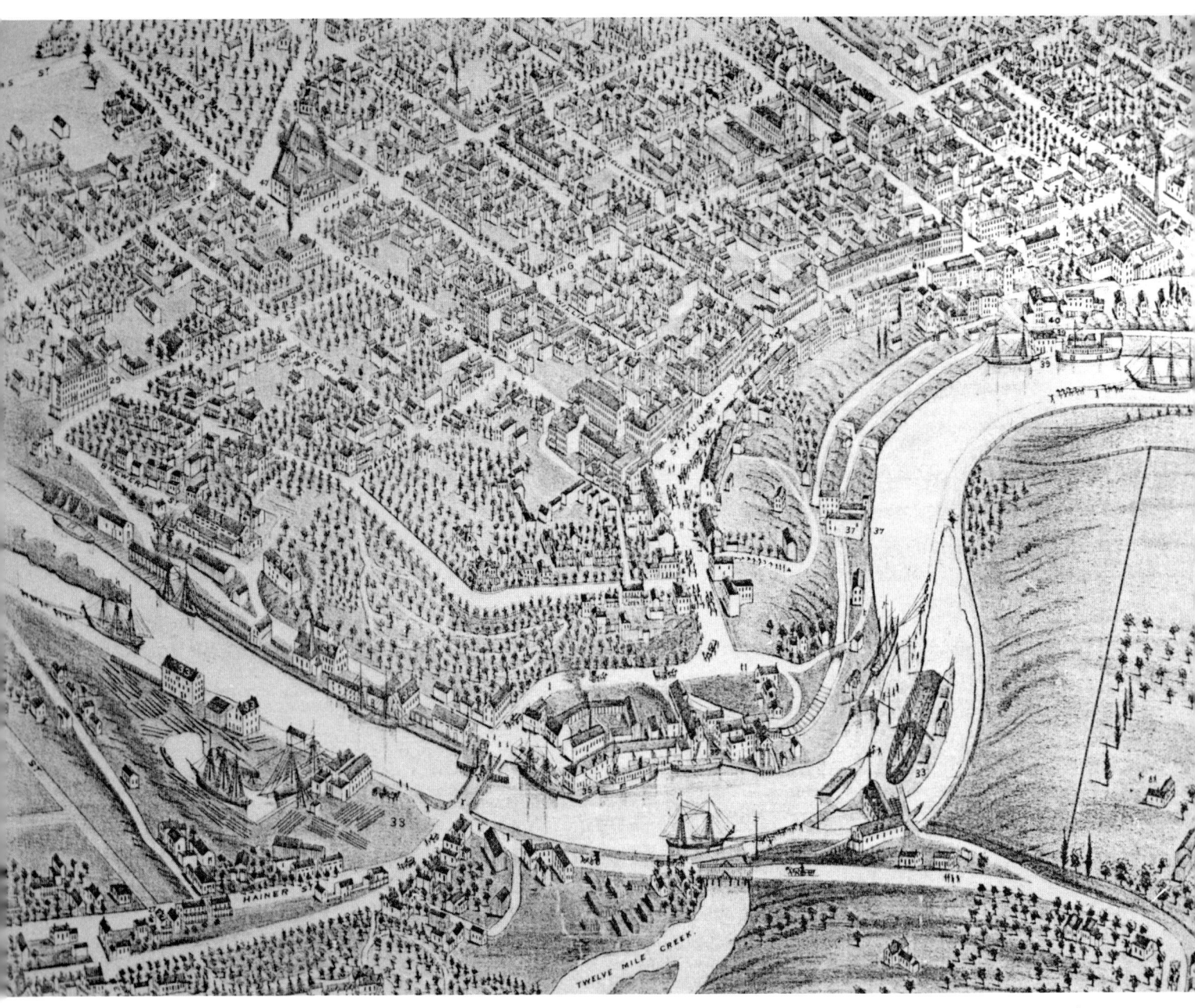

4.1 St. Catharines, ca. 1875: *Water supplied by the raceway, combined with pre-existing businesses, resulted in a concentration of industry on the St. Catharines – Thorold stretch of the canal. This detail from a bird's-eye view was intended to promote both the town and its industries, which are shown located mostly on the north side of the canal, since the towpath was on the opposite bank. The raceway is easily seen, running from the upper right and terraced into the hillside. Prominent enterprises are Shickluna's Shipyard, Drydock and Sawmill (33); Hunt, Cairns and Company Wheelworks (34); Norris' Wharf and Mills (35); Taylor and Bate's Brewery (36); Hutchinson's Mill (37); and the Dolphin Paint Works (40).* SCHM

4. INDUSTRY AND TRADE

Merritt and his colleagues built the First Welland Canal largely in order to improve the pioneer economy of an agricultural colony. They feared the growing prosperity of the Americans, and wanted to bring some of the trade from the Great Lakes settlements and the opening west to Upper Canada. Slowly but steadily, through recessions and depressions, they achieved their aims, to the point when, by 1850, 362,000 tonnes of goods were being carried through the canal annually [Fig. 1]. In 1856 a local journalist imagined unlimited growth, until "the whizzing noise and deafening buzz of ten thousand spindles and looms;...the splashing sounds of hundreds of water wheels, properly and advantageously worked,"[29] would be heard all along the waterway. Since his time, as we have seen, the canal has indeed grown in size, its locks and channel deepened and widened in order to accommodate the flood of raw materials and finished goods passing through. By 1961 the annual tonnage (metric) was 27,210,000; in 1980, nearly 54 million! The Welland system continued to grow during the competitive railway era, while the Erie Canal declined.

Before the opening of the prairies, south and southwest Ontario produced grain essential for local use, with sufficient surplus for export to Europe. The need to transform grain into flour contributed to the desire for a canal which would ensure steady power supplies. It is appropriate, then, that grain remains a staple cargo on the Welland Canal today. At first, cereal grains from Lake Erie ports made up the bulk of the downward traffic [Fig. 2], with coffee, furniture, sugar, molasses and earthenware comprising much of the upward-bound cargoes, heading west. One historian has described Upper Canada as a "barrel economy"[30] because most of these goods, as well as whisky, pork and beef, were transported in barrels, since this was the best way to transport liquids or perishables before refrigeration was invented [Fig. 3].

4.2 *The Farmers' Journal*, November 26, 1828.

4.3 The Barrel Economy: *Thousands of barrels once lined the wharves of Welland Canal ports, which resembled this imaginary harbour scene on a shipping receipt of the 1850s.*   SCHM: Norris-Neelon Papers

As the industrial revolution came to the Great Lakes area in the later 19th century, iron and steel manufacturing developed [Figs. 4, 5], so that soft coal and iron ore became common cargoes. Today, coal and coke, iron ore, wheat and other grains still make up the bulk of tonnage, along with fuel oil, and manufactured iron and steel [Fig. 6]. As part of the St. Lawrence Seaway (since 1959) the Welland Canal is like a giant funnel through which the goods of a large part of the North American continent pass.

If they could see it today, the original Welland Canal Company shareholders would be astonished at the wealth which moves through Niagara. They would also be amazed at the extent of development along the canal. Even in their own time, however, the canal-builders saw their "ditch" become an industrial corridor. In fact, in the mid-19th century there were even more mills and factories on the canal's banks than there are today! The waterway has seen a constantly changing industrial landscape, as mills were built, flourished and declined [Fig. 7]. Today amateur archaeologists delight in prowling through the remains of old stone mills in the canal towns, and professional industrial archaeologists have begun to seek out this fascinating area as part of the history of Canada's early industrial growth.

4.4 Thorold, ca. 1876: *On the Second Canal, between Locks 21 and 22, Dobbie's Iron and Brass Foundry (1865, Thorold's first foundry) provided jobs and brought business to the Escarpment-top town. The artist was much more interested in the mill's reflection than in the accurate portrayal of the horses, which are much too elegant! But he shared his contemporaries' love for one of the canal's "regulars" – the steam canaller PERSIA.* Page's Atlas

4.5 St. Catharines, ca. 1890 (opposite, top): *The Roller Mills of James Norris epitomize Second Canal prosperity at its height. In addition to the flour mills, the canal, its raceway and a number of ships can be seen, as well as the Grand Trunk Railway (crossing Twelve Mile Creek) in the distance. Norris, whose wealth was derived from the canal, became a shipowner and later a member of the St. Catharines' council, the mayor and M.P. for Lincoln County.* St. Catharines Centennial Library

4.6 The PIC RIVER, ca. 1970 (opposite, middle): *The PIC RIVER, seen on its way south to Lock 3 of the Fourth Canal, was equipped to carry either lumber and grain, or coal and iron ore. Here the 370-foot (113 m) long ship, active from 1896 to 1978, is carrying pulpwood.* Alfred F. Sagon-King

4.7 Thorold, ca. 1885: *A business established by Jacob Keefer (a son of George, first president of the Welland Canal Company), this thriving grist mill at Lock 24 of the Second Canal was the largest such mill in the Canadas when built in 1846. The handsome stone structure still stands, used for storage by Fraser Paper. Note the barrels!*
Metropolitan Toronto Library Board:
Ontario Gazetteer and Business Directory, 1884-85, p. 870

Initially, Merritt's idea was that a canal would provide a steady source of water for his own mill in St. Catharines. Other mill-owners had similar needs, and during construction, indeed until March 1831, the Canal Company offered free rights to water power to anyone who would build a mill on the new waterway. Later the Company leased these valuable rights. As early as 1830 the Canal provided water power for six mills, with four more under construction. By 1847 the Canal supported 32 saw- and grist-mills.[31]

The greatest concentration of industry on the First and Second Canals was in the Thorold-Merritton-St. Catharines area [see Fig. 1], where the change of levels and the steady flow of water passing over the Escarpment's brow provided the hydraulic power to turn a series of mill wheels [Fig. 8]. Additionally, this power potential was transferred down the waterway by a hydraulic raceway on the northeast side of the canal at the top of its bank [see Chap. 2, Fig. 15]. At St. Catharines this water, cascading down the bank in a series of waterfalls, was harnessed to drive more waterwheels. So great was the canal-based milling boom that older mill sites located about the Niagara peninsula quickly declined.

During the 1850s and 60s, however, flour-milling, sawmilling and the timber industry grew slowly, suffering occasionally from changes in the international tariff system. By the 1870s nearly every canal community had its lumber mill, however modest [Figs. 9, 10]. Woollen mills were also built, as well as rubber factories and shipbuilding enterprises. Clusters of these industries grew at all the canal communities [Fig. 10].

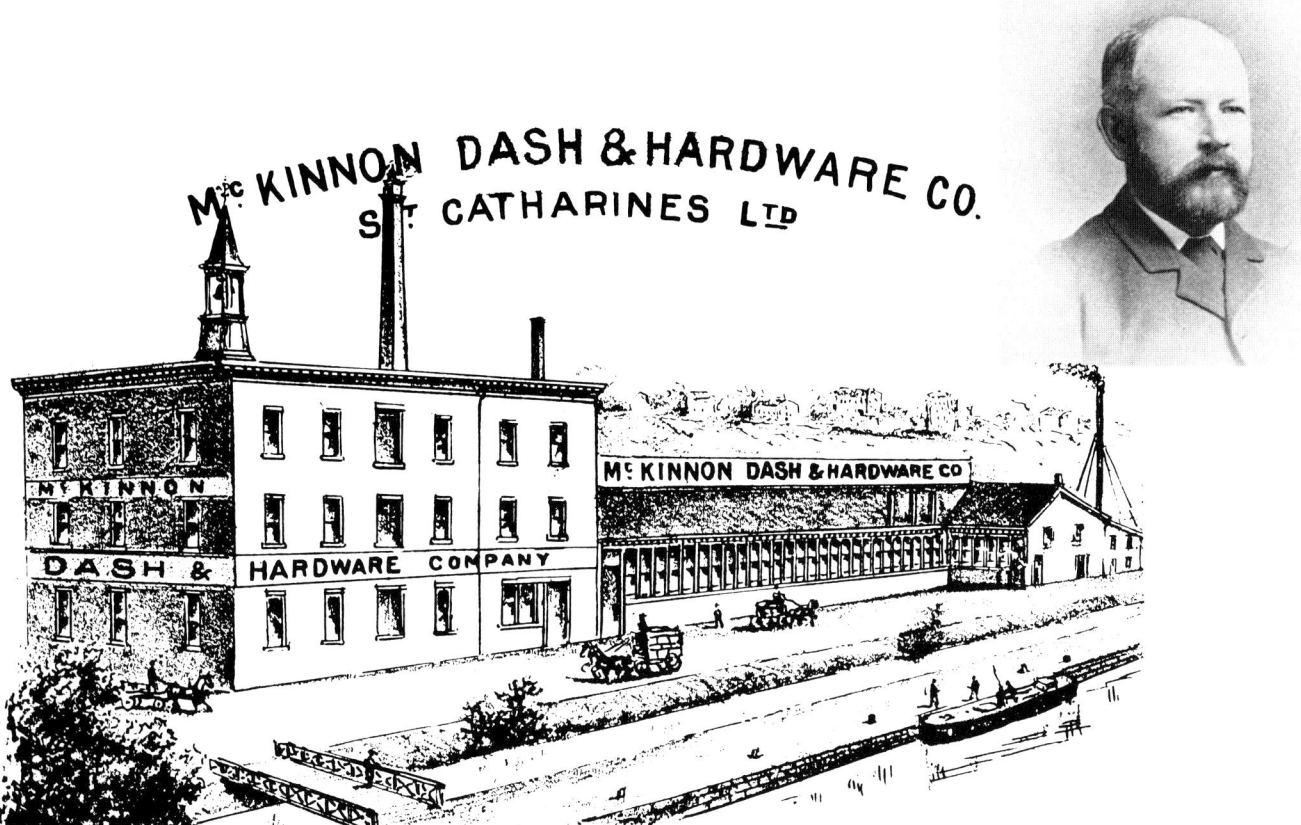

4.8 St. Catharines, ca. 1890: *Founded by Lachlan E. McKinnon (inset) in 1877, on the canalized Twelve Mile Creek, the business prospered until the 1930s Depression, when it was acquired by General Motors of Canada, who still operate plants on both Twelve Mile Creek and the Fourth Canal in St. Catharines. McKinnon, a hard-working Presbyterian from Owen Sound, was only one of the many entrepreneurs to whom canal-side industries brought success and wealth. In 1877 he formed McKinnon & Co., a carriage hardware business, out of which grew McKinnon Dash & Hardware Co., later a part of General Motors.*
St. Catharines Centennial Library; (inset) Men of Canada, Vol. 1, 1891

4.9 Welland, ca. 1876: *Mills such as Van Wyck and Johnson's Lumber and Planing Mill produced spokes, pails and broom handles, as well as planks, served shipbuilders and construction firms, and exported lumber.* Page's *Atlas*, p. 56

4.10 Merritton, ca. 1920: *Some of the lumber produced in the local mills was used in the manufacture of paper. Built in 1867, John Riordon's pulp and paper mill was one of the best equipped in North America. Located at Lock 18 of the Second Canal, it provided newsprint for Toronto's Globe, employment for hundreds, and economic growth for the settlement which had begun as "Slabtown."* SCHM: N-1042

This growth was assisted by the Welland Railway (opened in 1859) along the eastern canal bank, between Port Colborne and Port Dalhousie [Fig. 11]. It carried raw materials between the two ports, lightening the load of some ships too heavily laden to transit the canal otherwise, such as fully laden grain ships, which sat too low in the water to pass through the canal. They would have part of their cargoes removed before attempting entry into the canal, and part or all would be stored in an elevator prior to transshipment by rail [see, for example, Figs. 19, 20; Chap. 5, Figs. 1, 5]. The Welland Railway also linked the emerging industrial towns [see Chap. 7, Fig. 14], themselves just recently connected with the wider world through such east-west railways as the Grand Trunk.

4.11 Port Dalhousie, ca. 1885: *The Welland Railway station (centre), built in the popular "picturesque" style, was then still new. The grain elevator, built 1859, burned down in 1910. The EMPRESS OF INDIA, a side-wheeler, was too wide for the locks, so did not travel the canal.* SCHM: N-1586

4.12 and 13 St. Catharines, ca. 1890 (left, and opposite, top): *The Welland Vale Manufacturing Company played an important role in the symbiosis of town, countryside and canal. Located on an island in the canalized Twelve Mile Creek, near Lock 2 of the Second Canal (the lock is just out of sight, lower right), its works produced tools vital to local and Ontario farmers, and for export. It ceased operations only in 1965 and is now a campus of Niagara College. The advertisement appeared in the Gazetteer and Directory of the Great Western Railway of 1874.*

Metropolitan Toronto Library Board; SCHM: N-4237

Sleepy villages, in which previously the loudest noises had been the clip-clop of horses' hooves, the cries of children, and the ringing of church bells, were becoming "modern" industrial towns. The new mills required the building of wharves and jetties, swarming with horses, carts and carriages. They also created more jobs and attracted immigrants, so that strange accents and customs transformed the English-Scottish-Irish culture of the canal towns, resounding with the hoots of steam locomotives and factory whistles [Figs. 12, 13]. The already numerous pubs and hotels, some of whose "refreshments" were produced locally [Fig. 14], were filled with local and out-of-town (even out-of-country) customers, thanks to the thriving canal-based industries.

4.14 St. Catharines, ca. 1880: *Not all of the grain carried on the canal was destined for the flour mills; some was used for brewing. This site, across Twelve Mile Creek from Shickluna's shipyard, supported distilleries and breweries from 1834 to the 1930s. Note the schooner and scow — and the barrels!* SCHM: N-4057

To some, of course, the mills were a mixed blessing. The sawmills' owners dumped sawdust into the canal waters, clogging the weirs and locks at times of low water. Moreover, the first mills used some of the precious water needed to carry the ships. Particularly in the summer, the water level could be lowered by the hungry mill wheels to a dangerously shallow level. And so, mills and ships came into competition for the canal waters.

In the 1880s construction of the Third Canal brought some important changes to the industrial landscape. Certain enterprises disappeared: in Port Dalhousie, for example, the Andrews' dockyard was expropriated for a new Lock 1; and in Allanburg and Port Robinson, canal-widening devoured industrial sites. The stretch between Port Dalhousie and Thorold saw relatively little new industry along the new canal route since, to facilitate navigation, water rights were no longer leased.

Nevertheless, the water of the Second Canal and its raceway did continue to supply vital water power to mills in this area—including newcomers such as Willson Carbide in Merritton and the Provincial Paper Mill in Thorold [Fig. 15]. Lighting for the town of Thorold, as well as power for the Niagara, St. Catharines and Toronto Railway, were provided by a generating plant at Lock 24 [Fig. 16].

4.15 Thorold, ca. 1920: *After 1898 the Second Canal no longer carried traffic, but its hydraulic power was used until 1919. The Provincial Paper Mill (now Fraser Paper), centre, was located at Lock 23. A small flour mill, a spur line of the Welland Railway, a short raceway, and the local powerhouse can be seen in the lower part of the picture.* SCHM: N-3818

In the 20th century new heavy industry grew both at Port Colborne and Welland, in contrast to Port Dalhousie and Port Weller at the north end of the canal [Fig. 17]. Even in winter the canal was productive: until electric refrigerators became common, ice was harvested to supply community ice-boxes [Fig. 18]. Flour-milling, once the leading industry on the northern stretch of the canal, declined there and concentrated at Port Colborne, where it has remained [Figs. 19, 20].

4.16 Thorold, ca. 1910: *Lighting for the town of Thorold, as well as power for the Niagara, St. Catharines and Toronto Railway were provided from a generating plant on the Second Canal (left). The present Public Utilities Commission building is located here; George Keefer's mill is in the background. For the two weeks during each spring that the canal was drained for cleaning, the Railway had to revert to horses for power!*
John Burtniak Coll.

4.17 Port Colborne, ca. 1930: *A laker stops at the wharf of the Canadian Furnace Company, later used by the Algoma Central Railway.* John Burtniak Coll.

4.18 Port Colborne, ca. 1910: *Large ice blocks are put on a bucket conveyor, which will lift them into the icehouse, where they will be covered with sawdust to preserve them until the summer months. Many of the ice-merchants also dealt in wood and coal, a logical combination of seasonal businesses.* John Burtniak Coll.

4.19 and 20 Port Colborne, ca. 1910 (below) **and 1920** (opposite, top): *During the latter part of the 19th century, the skyline at the canal's southern terminus was dominated by the grain storage elevator of the Grand Trunk Railway. Tugs, sailing ships and freighters crowd the harbour; lumber cargoes are prominent, although grain was a major article of trade. Thrust into Lake Erie on reclaimed land the Government Elevator (left, built 1908, rebuilt following a 1919 explosion) and that of the Maple Leaf Milling Company (right, 1908) are still in operation.* John Burtniak Coll.

By the end of the 19th century, new forms of power, particularly hydro-electricity from Niagara Falls, replaced the canal as the major local source of power, but the canal corridor nevertheless remained industrial. New paper [Fig. 21], engineering works and metal-processing factories [Fig. 22] have developed along the waterway and in the canal communities — now grown from villages and towns into bustling industrial centres. Although not all of these communities still use the canal's facilities, they had become established because of the railway and highway connections, and the earlier industries and services which had been the creation of the waterway [Figs. 23, 24].

4.21 Thorold, ca. 1980 (below): *The Ontario Paper Company Mill, established on the Third Canal in 1912. When the Fourth Canal was built the company expanded, building its own wharves and turning basin. It is now the fifth largest producer of newsprint in North America.*   Ontario Paper Co.

4.22 Port Colborne, ca. 1920: *Opened in 1918, the International Nickel Company (INCO) brought a new skyline feature to this busy harbour, and a new form of pollution. The refinery used nickel ore from Sudbury. Under one roof, its structures cover 23 acres (nearly 10 hectares). Through the middle of the picture run the Third and Fourth Canals with their characteristic lift bridges.* PAC: PA-15635

4.23 St. Catharines, ca. 1885: *By this time the Second Canal (curving at the right) had been replaced by the Third, which by-passed the city. But St. Paul Street still boasted businesses with far-flung connections. Signs on the building third from the left advertised an Atlantic shipping company.* SCHM: N-1027

A quiet agrarian corner of Upper Canada became a vital part of North America's industrial network — thanks to Merritt's ditch.

4.24 St. Catharines: *Businessman and shipowner Captain Sylvester Neelon built this house on King Street in 1862, evidence of the wealth the Second Canal had brought to canal communities, and lending a touch of elegance to the still somewhat rugged pioneer community. Many of Neelon's ships were built in the St. Catharines' shipyard of Louis Shickluna and in the Andrews' yard in Port Dalhousie. Neelon was but one of many who built impressive homes out of their canal-related profits; most, however, chose sites overlooking the waterway.* R.R. Taylor

5.1 Port Colborne, ca. 1860 (above): *In the foreground are the winches and gates of Lock 27 of the Second Canal, with a characteristic white swing bridge. In the background is the Grand Trunk Railway's grain storage elevator.* PCHMM

5.2 Port Dalhousie, 1882 (below): *At the Muir Brothers Dry Dock near Lock 1, work proceeds on scraping the hull of the yacht ORIOLE (on the left) and refitting of a steam propellor (right). In the distance is Martindale Pond, with its floating towpaths, and on the left the entrance to the then new Third Canal, with the mouth of Twelve Mile Creek in the centre. Behind the camera is the port itself, and Lake Ontario.*
SCHM: N-1051

5. SHIPS AND SHIPBUILDING

"I have seen strings of schooners wending their way from lock to lock, resembling a floating forest at a distance," said a letter in the *St. Catharines Journal* in 1842. The description is typical of mid-19th-century canal ports, with the masts of canallers, barks, and brigs from the Great Lakes and Atlantic, for ships have always been as important a part of the Welland Canal as have been the locks and lock gates designed to facilitate their passage, and the spillways and weirs which control the water supply [Fig. 1]. For over a century and a half ships have carried raw materials and finished products through the waterway, to and from the industries along its banks. The ships have been pulled and pushed, proceeded under their own power, repaired and serviced, moored, piloted – and even built – along the Welland Canal.

As early as the 1820s small inland towns, remote from the ocean and far even from lakes Erie and Ontario, had begun to construct vessels for operation on the canal, and in the wider world beyond. For much of the 19th century, shipbuilding boomed along the canals, with as many as eight drydocks [Fig. 2] and several shipbuilding yards operating in the industry's heyday. No canal community was without its entrepreneurs, carpenters, metal workers and other skilled artisans. The construction of wooden sailing ships, canal barges and later steel freighters produced employment, stimulated the economy and gave character to the canal towns.

5.3 St. Catharines, ca. 1864: *Near Lock 3 both the "old" (a barkentine) and the "new" (a steam-powered canaller) are being constructed at the inner basin of Shickluna's shipyard. On the other side of the canalized Twelve Mile Creek can be seen Taylor's Brewery, the comfortable homes on Yates Street (named for one of the First Canal's financiers), and the fashionable Stephenson House spa – signs of St. Catharines' prosperity.*
SCHM: N-2795

By 1827 Russell Armington had begun to repair and build ships on an island in Twelve Mile Creek between Port Dalhousie and St. Catharines. Armington was encouraged by William Hamilton Merritt, to whom the shipyard reverted when Armington became ill in the mid-1830s. In 1838 this pioneer yard was leased by the Maltese shipbuilder Louis Shickluna, who in 1841 moved his yard to a site between Locks 2 and 3 (i.e., closer to St. Catharines). There, for nearly 40 years, Shickluna built schooners, barkentines and brigantines (all sailing ships), as well as steam propellors, barges and tugs [Fig. 3]. At Lock 3, in 1850, he established a drydock to meet the rising demand for ship repairs. Before he died in 1880, Shickluna had supervised the construction of over one hundred different vessels.

In the 1860s Melancthon Simpson established a shipyard at Lock 5 on the Second Canal (also in St. Catharines), having previously built ships elsewhere [Fig. 4]. Among those built by Simpson was the well-known steam canaller, the PERSIA [see Fig. 9]. Simpson also operated a shipyard on the Welland River, just east of the lock at Port Robinson.

Shipbuilding was an industry extremely sensitive to the development of the waterway and to changes in technology [Fig. 5]. In St. Catharines, for example, shipbuilding enterprises declined after the construction of the Third Canal, which by-passed the city's industrial heart. Here and elsewhere in the area, the viability of larger vessels, the introduction of steam power and iron hulls (replacing sail and wood), and other technological developments helped to cause the near demise of local shipbuilding.

For longer than any others, the Muir Brothers Dry Dock was located near Lock 1 of the Second Canal in Port Dalhousie [see Fig. 2]. From 1850, when they built their remarkable floating drydock, to the 1890s, they constructed many types of vessel, including schooners and the timber "droghers" (with ports or doors in the stern for loading). They continued to repair ships on the same site until 1954. On the east side of the harbour, Anderson and Andrews were building ships in the 1860s and 1870s, in competition with Alexander Muir and his brothers.

5.4 St. Catharines, 1874: *Melancthon Simpson's advertisement suggests the interdependence of lumber mills and shipbuilding, as well as the predominance of steam by the 1870s. As a matter of fact, Simpson never built any vessel of the type shown in the advertisement!* SCHM

5.5 Port Colborne, 1885: *Lake schooners traditionally had flared bows and wide transoms, but their "cousins," the early wooden canallers (built to fit the canal locks) had boxlike hulls.* PAC: C-757

Port Dalhousie and St. Catharines had no monopoly over the industry. At Port Robinson, in addition to Melancthon Simpson, John P. and James S. Abbey built fine barkentines [Fig. 6], while William Ross and his sons constructed tugs. Alfred White was also in business there, as well as in Thorold, Welland and Humberstone. At Welland, Matthew Beatty specialized in dredges [see Fig. 21], while George Hardison had a shipyard at Port Colborne. On a lesser scale, ships were also built at Dunnville, where the Feeder Canal met the Grand River.

5.6 Port Robinson, 1874: *The shipyard of John P. Abbey built the CITY OF ST. CATHARINES, a steam canaller, in 1874. His yard stood between the lock connecting the canal with the Welland River and the Welland Railway line, strategically located between three modes of communication and trade.*
Mrs. F.A. Goldspink/Fred A. Addis

Today major shipbuilding, repair and maintenance are carried on only at Port Weller, the Lake Ontario terminus [Fig. 7]. In 1937 a drydock was constructed near Lock 1 of the then new Fourth Canal for repairing the waterway's floating equipment. A private company took over the enterprise in 1946 and still operates it today — on land once owned by the Muir brothers! At the other end of the canal, ship repair and dismantling are still carried on at Port Colborne, especially in the slack winter months when the canal itself is closed [see Fig. 23].

In the early canal days, the ships were sailing vessels, usually schooners, but also some brigs and barkentines, which had to be towed by horses along the channel [see Preface, Fig. 1; Chap. 4, Fig. 1]. The variable winds could drive a sailing vessel violently against lock walls or canal banks, or leave her totally becalmed. Vessels built at canal-side shipyards were often specifically designed to fit efficiently into the locks. Early "canallers" were usually about 110 feet (34 m) long, the length of a First Canal lock. To secure maximum capacity, their hulls were boxlike, and their bows and sterns rose almost vertically above the water. All had to fit neatly into the locks' dimensions and rise or descend without being damaged as the water level changed, so spars could not protrude beyond the vessels' sides [Fig. 8].

When the first steamships appeared on the canal, they could make their way through the locks under their own power [Fig. 9]. At first built of wood, these sturdy canallers (known as propellors) would often carry passengers (in cabins above their cargo decks). By about 1850 *iron* canallers began replacing the earlier types and for almost a century were common sights, with their blunt bows and wheelhouses forward [Fig. 10]. However, particularly since the opening of the new St. Lawrence Seaway canal system in 1959, they have become outmoded and replaced by even larger vessels [Figs. 11, 12].

5.7 Port Weller, 1950: *The Port Weller Dry Docks Limited, near Lock 1, is the last great shipyard on the canal. It has built bulk freighters, tugs, barges, dredges, icebreakers and passenger vessels. Remodelling, reconstruction and occasionally scrapping of ships are also undertaken.* SCHM: N-3232

5.8 Port Dalhousie, 1878: *Many of these ships — such as the barkentine ARK in the left foreground — were built by the Muir brothers. Others in the outer harbour may have been built at other canal ports. The ARK's cargo of lumber was a staple item of 19th-century canal and lake commerce.* SCHM: N-1014

5.9 St. Catharines, 1880: *Steam replaces sail: the steam canaller PERSIA and the barque EMERALD, built by Melancthon Simpson and George Hardison respectively, take on cargo. Both have the rectangular, boxlike hulls suitable for lock passage. The EMERALD had been built specifically for the timber trade and had stern doors which opened for loading.*

AO: S-15995

As demand for increased cargo capacity has continued through the years, changes in both size and design of ships has been necessary, and these changes in turn have forced periodic enlargements of both the channel and locks of the canal itself.

5.10 Port Colborne, 1929: *At the opening of Lock 8 of the Fourth Canal, three steel canallers await passage inland. Their shallow draught and extended length had been ideal for the locks of the Third Canal. The larger locks of the "new" waterway were both a response and an invitation to wider and longer ships.*
SCHM: N-6783

5.11 Thorold, 6 August 1932 (below): *The Western world was in the depths of the Great Depression, but the Niagara Peninsula, and Canada as a whole, had something to celebrate: the new, ultra-modern Welland Canal. The star performer at the official opening was the LEMOYNE, then the largest ship on the Great Lakes, seen here at Lock 7, beflagged for the ceremonies. Some of the admiring crowd have been temporarily diverted by the official photographer!* PAC: PA-49787

5.12 Port Robinson, 1972 (above): *The CANADIAN CENTURY, a "self-unloader," constructed at Port Weller in 1967, has a built-in series of cargo-handling belts which can lift the ship's contents to deck level, from which a boom transfers them to the wharf. Despite this ingenious development, this coal-carrier is still recognizably a "laker."* Alfred F. Sagon-King

5.13 St. Catharines, ca. 1906 : *Steam-powered tugs became a common sight on the Third Canal. The AUGUSTA is shown towing the schooner-barge ANNIE PETERSON through Lock 3, at an elegant bridge near Ontario Street.*
Inland Seas, 1964, p. 224

Although exotic vessels occasionally have been seen on the waterway [see Chap. 9], ships built on the canal, and most of those seen passing through, have been sturdy workhorses [Fig. 13]. For example, while modern ships usually make their way through the canal under their own power, there is still a role for tugboats, which push or pull barges, and which are still active around ship repair yards. Less glamorous than the cargo-carrying vessels, and less picturesque than the towhorses and towboys they replaced during the Third Canal era, the new "workhorses" were used extensively during the building of the Third Canal, pulling dredges, scows and other floating construction equipment [Figs. 14, 15; see also Fig. 4]. Working scows [Fig. 16] and barges [Figs. 17, 18] have also had a continuing part to play in the workaday world of the canals.

5.14 Thorold, January 1977 (above): *These two modern tugs are at the end of Lock 7, leaving the stretch of canal about to be de-watered for the winter, temporarily retired from service.*   Alfred F. Sagon-King

5.15 Near Thorold, 1979 (opposite, top): *Shunters, a variation of the tug, move an upbound laker between Locks 3 and 4. Development of shunters was an unsuccessful experiment in the ongoing attempt to expedite the movement of ever-larger ships through the canal.*   Alfred F. Sagon-King

5.16 Port Colborne, ca. 1930: *Working scows are prominent in the foreground of this view, taken from the highway lift bridge. The Fourth Canal was not yet completed, and the still-functioning Third Canal is at the right. The harbour had been recently excavated and is full of ships.* PAC: PA-48168

5.17 Port Colborne, 1924: *As with the canal itself, and the ships which use it, barges have also grown in size and sophistication. The construction barges at Port Colborne in 1924 were small and simple indeed compared with the huge barge ENERGY FREEDOM (see Fig. 18).* PAC: PA-86886

Another type of craft essential to the passage of ships through the canal is the pilot boat, since the officers of many vessels are not familiar with canal conditions and currents in the various segments of the system [Fig. 19]. Beginning with the Third Canal, constant dredging has been necessary, particularly as the draft of ships became deeper and traffic increased, thus bringing yet another type of "workhorse" to the scene [Figs. 20, 21].

5.19 Port Weller, ca. 1970: *The pilot boat QU'APPELLE heads out of harbour, taking a pilot to a waiting ship needing guidance through the system: perhaps an ocean-going "saltie" whose officers are not sufficiently familiar with canal conditions.* SCHM: N-6883

5.18 Thorold, 1981: *Like all barges, the ENERGY FREEDOM (seen here being pushed through Lock 4) has no means of propulsion and is unable to move unless towed or pushed by either a tug or a freighter.*
Mike Conley, St. Catharines *Standard*

5.20 Port Colborne, ca. 1882: *This rather primitive dredge, built of wood, is being tended by a steam tug. Note in the background the Grand Trunk Railway grain elevator (left) and the breakwater with its lighthouse (centre).* Picturesque Canada, 1882

5.21 Welland, ca. 1900: *The DREDGE PRIMROSE, built by Matthew Beatty and Sons of Welland, was a much more sophisticated version of an essential canal workhorse than that shown in Fig. 20. The company specialized in a variety of equipment designed for maintenance and reconstruction of the waterway, not merely dredges. Irish-born William Beatty had settled in Thorold in 1834, obtained a mill privilege from the Welland Canal Company, and went into the lumber business with tanning as a sideline.* SCHM: N-1188

In this chapter we have illustrated only some of the more common types of vessels on the canal, vessels which not only have grown larger over the decades, but also reflect the changing nature of the commerce they carry and the services required to keep them safely afloat [Figs. 22, 23].

Such ships, and those who build, maintain and operate them, have helped to provide employment for thousands and at the same time have given the canal towns their special character as "inland ports."

5.22 Port Weller, 1954 – An Auspicious Beginning: *The SCOTT MISENER, a typical modern laker of the Misener Transportation fleet, about to be christened at the fit-out berth: an occasion for celebration.* SCHM: N-6243

5.23 Ramey's Bend, 1977 – An Ignominious End: *Between Port Colborne and Welland, part of the abandoned Third Canal today provides an ideal spot for dismantling outdated or irreparable vessels: a "ships' graveyard" for hard-working and far-ranging ships, many of which had been built in the once bustling yards of canal-side communities.* Alfred F. Sagon-King

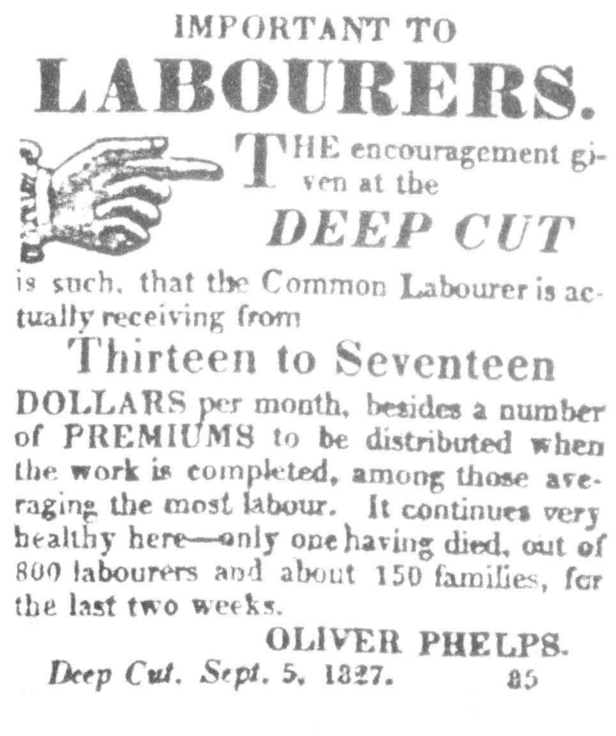

IMPORTANT TO LABOURERS.

THE encouragement given at the **DEEP CUT** is such, that the Common Labourer is actually receiving from **Thirteen to Seventeen** DOLLARS per month, besides a number of PREMIUMS to be distributed when the work is completed, among those averaging the most labour. It continues very healthy here—only one having died, out of 800 labourers and about 150 families, for the last two weeks.

OLIVER PHELPS.

Deep Cut, Sept. 5, 1827.   85

6.1 St. Catharines, 1827 (left): *As many as 800 unskilled workers were employed digging the channels for the First and Second Canals. They were underpaid, often sick, and quite often slightly drunk, fuelled by the "grog-man" – an employee regularly on the Canal Company's paylist. The reference to "very healthy" conditions was false advertising!*
St. Johns Outdoor Studies Centre

6.2 Scottish Stonecutters, 1870s-80s (below): *These men were an important new element in the canal area, brought in to prepare the huge limestone blocks required for the locks of the Third Canal (1874-1887).*
SCHM: L967.112.5

6. CREATING EMPLOYMENT

Despite crude or complex machinery, despite increasingly sophisticated ships, despite improvements in working conditions, the Welland Canals have been built, maintained, operated and serviced by human energy [Fig. 1]. In this respect they have provided, directly or indirectly, a myriad of jobs for thousands in the canal-related communities [Fig. 2].

Nevertheless, the story of employment on the canals did not begin happily. The hundreds of men — mostly Irish — who built the first two canals worked in circumstances utterly appalling to the modern reader (or worker!). Although we lack pictorial evidence of working conditions then, we do have verbal descriptions. For example, we are told that, about 1825, men on the construction sites:

> …subsisted on the coarsest fare, holding their lives as uncertain as those of the leaders of a forlorn hope. Men excluded from all the advantages of civilization, often at the mercy of a hard contractor, who wrung his profits from their blood — blasting rocks, digging in the hard clay, uprooting trees, clearing the ground of briars — and doing all this for a pittance that merely enabled them to exist. The fetid exhalations arising from the pestilential swamps in which they were working produced diseases unknown and unheard of in their own country. The Irish labourers of those days stood in trenches up to the knees in water and mire, and the putrid exhalations rising from the earth consumed them with fever or set their teeth chattering as with cold, while the sweat rolled from their foreheads. They waded knee deep in black muck, wheeled, dug, hewed, bore heavy burdens on their shoulders, exposed at all times to every change of temperature, till stricken down with fever, they took refuge in the shanties, and in narrow bunks trembled with disease.[32]

Excessive drinking was a fact of life among the workers, partly because local water supplies were unfit for consumption, especially in the marshes. To quench the labourers' thirst, "waterboys" regularly passed through the ranks, serving whisky from tin pails, using tin dippers. Not surprisingly, violence and accidents were commonplace.

In such conditions, the men who built the first two canals had to work with picks, shovels, scrapers and plows to loosen the earth, then shovel it (without benefit of steam- or gas-powered engines) into wheelbarrows, which they pushed themselves, and then into ox-drawn carts or horse-drawn wagons for transport to various "fills" at some distance from the excavation site. Mud was often removed from the site in bags slung over the men's shoulders, in wheelbarrows or in wagons drawn by oxen, horses or mules: back-breaking labour for the men, and dangerous for both the men and animals, many of which were killed sliding down slippery ditch banks [Fig. 3]. Rock had to be drilled by hand and blasted apart with gunpowder, then primitively transported. Needless to say accidents were numerous.

As we have seen (Chapter 3), the equipment and expertise required for even such primitive construction methods were not available in Upper Canada in 1824, when "Mr. Merritt's ditch" was begun. Fortunately for his plans, work on the Erie Canal was almost finished, and the canal contractors were more than pleased to bring their ox-teams, iron plows and harrows, and their experience in excavating, to a new site across the border. It was they, with their ability to follow the instructions of the supervising engineers, who would build the locks, dams, culverts and towpaths required.

No wonder that the Irish, described as "strong, sturdy, and not afraid of hard work,"[33] were in demand – particularly those with horses or oxen. But they were paid only $10-13 a month, and lived in boarding houses at $1.50 a week (almost half a man's weekly wage) or, if they had families (as many did), in flimsy shanties. By 1827, as the First Canal was nearing completion, average wages had risen to $12-14; a man with his own team could command $15-18, and one with two yoke of oxen and a stout cart could get up to $26.[34] In addition, each of the 35 sections into which the canal had been divided required 12-15 shovellers, one overseer (the best might be paid as much as $100 a month), and 5-6 teams of horses.

A special role was played by the Irish, not only in the 1820s, but also during the 1840s. Following completion of the canal in 1829, many of those who had come from New York for the work had remained in the area as teamsters. In the 1840s they were joined by several thousand of their compatriots for the rebuilding of the canal with locks of stone. Cessation of improvements on the Erie Canal (April 1842) once again provided a work force for the Welland. But this time unemployed workers from the canal operations on the St. Lawrence swelled the numbers of men looking for work on the canal. In addition, immigrants were arriving in a steady stream directly from Ireland. The competition among these groups for a limited number of jobs was intensified by Old-Country feuds which they maintained in the New World.

6.3 England, 1830s: *Specific facts about labourers on the First and Second Canals are hard to find, and pictorial representations are virtually nonexistent, but this sketch by J.C. Bourne (to illustrate conditions on the London and Birmingham Railway) probably gives a fair indication of the equipment and conditions which prevailed on early 19th-century construction sites in North America – excluding the steam engine, of course!* Elton Coll., Ironbridge Gorge Museum Trust

As the Canal Company (and its occasionally unscrupulous contractors) struggled to make ends meet, the labourers suffered, especially in winter. Not having the means or opportunity to become farmers, they endured seasonal unemployment. Along with the execrable working conditions on the canal, they faced disease (malaria, cholera, and typhoid), lack of a stable home life (wives and children were constantly having to move from camp to camp), and the aforementioned feuds.

Too many applicants for too few jobs, added to the ghastly working and living conditions, fueled the tensions, and on a number of occasions during 1842 and 1849 violence erupted [Fig. 4]. While a minority took to violence, the majority made a positive contribution to the canal communities. For example, Irish workers donated their labour to help build the church (later Cathedral) of St. Catherine of Alexandria [Fig. 5]. Ultimately, most of the Irish settled down in the area and became good citizens.

6.4 Merritton, 1849 (above): *Pariahs to the well-bred Loyalist establishment, the Irish took a long time to settle in; and at one stage some had been confined in camps surrounded by high fences with locked gates! Old antagonisms and a continuing sense of exclusion from society bred frustration, which erupted into violence on more than one occasion. The sketch portrays Duffin's Inn, in "Slabtown" (later part of Merritton), the scene of a shootout between Irish Orangemen and Irish Catholics on 12 July 1849. Two men were left dead.*

St. Johns Outdoor Studies Centre; SCHM: N-1055

6.5 St. Catharines, 1976 (right): *The Cathedral of St. Catherine of Alexandria (built between 1843 and 1845) has in the narthex a stone tablet bearing this dedication (in translation): "To God, the Greatest and the Best, and under the invocation of the Blessed Catherine, Virgin and Martyr, the Irish working on the Welland Canal built this monument of faith and piety, 1844." Its spire is still a landmark in the city where the canal idea was born.*   R.R. Taylor

While it was mainly the Irish who built the first two canals, by the late 19th and early 20th centuries conditions in other parts of Europe were pushing thousands of people to seek their fortunes elsewhere. Large-scale construction projects in North America continued to act as magnets, hence the labour force for construction of the Third and Fourth Canals included Scots, Poles, Italians and Finns, to name only a few of the new immigrants [Fig. 6]. The canal-side towns owe at least some of their ethnic diversity to these successive waves of immigration. Many of the newcomers (like the Irish before them) found continued employment in the various industries and services connected with the canal's operation, as, for example, lockmasters, locktenders, drydock and shipyard workers.

6.6 Near Thorold, 1914: *On the Fourth Canal, Italians were among the newcomers. Working near Lock 4, this group is laying the tracks vital for locomotives bringing cars loaded with building materials.* PAC: PA-61139

Technological and medical innovations made work on the Third Canal less rigorous than previously. But despite such advances, men using scrapers were still an important element of the workforce, as were the horse-drawn carts – even in the early stages of construction of the Fourth Canal [Figs. 7, 8].

6.7 Third Welland Canal, ca. 1880 (opposite, top): *The work site was by no means pleasant, even in the 1880s, especially as the larger structures and equipment began to dwarf the labourers.* SCHM: N-3967

6.8 Near Port Weller, 1915 (opposite, bottom): *Between the future sites of Locks 1 and 2 of the Fourth Canal (south of what became Port Weller), men and horses wait with their wagons to haul off spoil (clay, etc.) from the deepening channel, as they had since the earliest days of canal-building. The cart drivers would take their loads down to Port Weller, where the spoil would help to build piers for the new harbour.*
SCHM: N-1001

When construction resumed after World War I, small steam shunter locomotives were available (faster than horses), but digging the channel was still arduous labour [Fig. 9]. Nevertheless the work, while just as dusty, boring and dangerous as before [Fig. 10], was by then safer and less demeaning – and wages, of course, were much improved. From the surveyors [Fig. 11] to the men who built the huge steel lock gates, the men who constructed the canals did not have an easy or pleasant task, especially before the arrival of the 40-hour week and medicare [Fig. 12].

6.9 Fourth Canal, ca. 1925 (above): *Workers taking a much deserved breather from still arduous labour seem proud to be associated with the little steam shunter.*
SCHM: N-5008

6.10 Port Weller, ca. 1928 (left): *Building an underground conduit (under Lock 1), grimy but sturdy workers resembled coal miners and were engaged in equally difficult and dangerous work. One hundred and eighteen such men were killed building the Fourth Canal [see Chap. 9, Fig. 16].*
PAC: C-33930

6.11 Near Port Weller, 1911: *Laying out the route of the Fourth Canal, near what would become Port Weller, these surveyors found that a broadbrimmed hat kept them cool – and that a horse was still the best transportation over uneven farmland.*
St. Catharines Centennial History

6.12 Port Weller, 1927: *Some of the "unsung heroes" of canal construction, these men are building – on site – one of the largest lock gates on the Fourth Canal, at Lock 1. Dwarfed by its immense latticework, they are at the mercy of wind and weather.* PAC: C-33922

91

From the beginning, the engineers, contractors, overseers, teamsters and shovellers engaged in the actual construction were only a part of the army of builders. All those involved (and their families) had to be housed [Fig. 13], fed and clothed. The animals, too, required shelter and provisioning—and the services of blacksmiths, harness-makers and carpenters to maintain the animals and carts. All of these activities created additional jobs.

6.13 Accommodation, Fourth Canal: *The Department of Railways and Canals, responsible for the building of the Fourth Canal, provided temporary accommodation for construction workers—a far cry from the hovels and shanties in which the First Canal labourers had to dwell [and see Fig. 14].*   SCHM: N-1995

6.14 Merritton, 1980: *Responding to the need for both social stability in canal towns and efficiency in operating the canal (not yet a booming enterprise), in the 1850s the government built homes such as these for locktenders and their families. Located a few yards from the locks (here, the flight of locks along Bradley Street), such houses were built of sturdy sandstone from local quarries. These particular ones are still inhabited.*
R.R. Taylor

In addition, facilities for the termini and intermediate ports were necessary: wharves, docks, housing for lockmasters and locktenders [Fig. 14], customs houses [Fig. 15], and ship services, such as sailmakers and chandlers in the early days. The towboys ("boys" whatever their age) and their animals, so crucial in the days of sail, had to be provided with accommodation at intervals of a day's travel. Hence "service" centres developed at certain points along the waterway, creating the villages, towns and eventually the cities, which are shown in Chapter 7.

The canal itself, as well as its passing ships, required ongoing servicing. Immigrants to the area found work maintaining the channel, locks and towpaths, repairing vessels, provisioning ships, constructing canal boats or providing towing facilities with horseteams and later tugboats. Locks and bridges had to be operated on a daily basis at least eight months of the year, giving rise to the occupations of locktenders and lockmasters. Offices were established to exact tolls, dues and customs levies from the ships at official points of entry, and a canal "bureaucracy" evolved. Newcomers also arrived to work in the industries which developed to process raw materials into finished goods, and to market both such local products and goods imported from elsewhere on the canal's ships.

6.15 Port Dalhousie, ca. 1878: *Several canal towns were official ports of entry to Canada, and so government bureaucracy provided "white collar" jobs for customs officials. This collectors' office near Lock 1 of the Second Canal probably also housed locktenders and their families.* AO: Acc. 12026-60

The four canals, as construction projects, are themselves monuments to human skill and endurance. But repair and maintenance of the canal have also been a continuing source of employment, requiring equally talented and courageous individuals [Figs. 16, 17]. Even in the freezing conditions of the winter months, the canal requires attention, since it is then that the locks must be repaired and made ready for the spring re-opening [Figs. 18, 19].

6.16 **Near Thorold, 1955**: *More unsung heroes, working under the huge gates at Lock 7. Notice the heavy rivetted steel [see Chap. 9, Fig. 1].* PAC: C-34857

6.17 **Port Colborne, ca. 1907-08**: *Not all canal-created jobs were on or near the canal. Posing proudly with his underwater equipment (and his wife), Donald Fletcher of Port Colborne represents another technological development: the ability to work in the canal.* PCHMM: P972-758

While construction and maintenance workers are essential to the operation of any canal, so too are those who tend the locks, and the men (and women!) who crew the ships [Figs. 20, 21].

6.18 Fourth Canal, ca. 1980 (above, left): *Sleet and snow can add to the difficulties of the surveyor's job!*
Buffalo and Erie County Historical Society

6.19 Port Weller, 1980 (above, right): *At Lock 1 the guard gates are closed, the channel is drained, and winter repairs are under way. Workers are dwarfed by giant equipment and towering lock walls. Nowadays, many ships are almost too large for the 50-year-old canal and strike the lock walls, damaging the concrete; the maintenance work never ceases [and see Chap. 9, Fig.12].* R.R. Taylor

6.20 Third Canal, ca. 1908 (left): *The locktender at Lock 4 found that the electrically powered gates saved effort and gave him a chance to study the ships passing through [see Chap. 3, Fig. 5, for hand-operation of early canal gates].* OA: Murphy Collection (3)

6.21 St. Catharines, ca. 1975 (above): *A "space-age" system of closed-circuit TV (with special cameras for night visibility), unmanned microwave detectors, videographs, and other equipment for weather observation, and a videoscope recorder for unusual conditions or events — all this (and more) is used to control today's ship traffic. Such sophisticated devices (at the St. Lawrence Seaway Headquarters, Western Region) would have amazed the towboys of the First and Second (and the locktenders of the first three) Canals.*
St. Lawrence Seaway Authority: Western Region

6.22 St. Catharines, ca. 1857 (left): *The object of the canal, then as now, was to move ships and their cargoes, and crewing the ships has provided seasonal employment for thousands of men since 1829. This sailor (from a receipt in the files of Captain Sylvester Neelon's St. Catharines-based company, 1857) is idealized, but the barrel and bale at his feet recall the types of cargo on the early canals.*
SCHM: Norris-Neelon Papers

In the new communities, the saw- and flour mills, whose profitable year-round operation was the *raison d'être* of the canal, multiplied rapidly, and they in turn required builders, operators, wheelwrights, coopers and the like [Figs. 22, 23]. White-collar workers, too, found employment: bookkeepers, clerks, surveyors, accountants — all had vital roles to play, as levels and surveys, leases and other legal documents and services required the development of a growing bureaucratic and professional class. As well, schools were needed, and churches were established to satisfy the spiritual needs of the rapidly increasing population. Not to mention the numerous taverns, supplied at least in part by local industry [Fig. 24].

For continuing groups of newcomers, then, the canals have created a livelihood, happily in steadily improving conditions. As the first shantytowns became more stable, they developed into nine prospering communities – created by the canal.

6.23 Welland, ca. 1890: *These foundry men and machinists were employed by Robertson Brothers. Their mill (founded 1879) produced steam- as well as horse-powered hoists, ploughs, derrick fittings and other equipment for the canal, local industry and agriculture: an enterprise created by the canal, and serving the wider community of the Niagara Peninsula.*
Welland Public Library

6.24 St. Catharines, ca. 1925: *Before the days of a safe water supply, beer provided a common alternative. Hence processing the by-products of grain provided employment for many in various canal-side towns. Near the northern end of the canal, the Taylor and Bate Brewery was still employing a large staff when this picture was taken. The canal was at the left; Yates Street is up the hill to the right; Highway 406 now runs straight through this site.* SCHM: N-1407

7.1 St. Catharines, 1850: *Founded by United Empire Loyalists in the 1790s, the village was originally called "The Twelve" (after the Creek) and "Shipman's Corners" (after Paul Shipman, a well-known tavern owner and an early supporter of the canal). This view, painted shortly after the village's incorporation as a town, shows the canal-creek confluence, the ubiquitous mills and warehouses, and the Taylor brewery (7). The skyline reveals the affluence and sophistication already achieved: the Stephenson House spa (1), and the homes of Merritt (2) and Dr. Theophilus Mack (3), an Irish-born developer of the salt springs. In 1976 centennial celebrations made use of a symbolic representation of a ship in the canal [inset], a reminder of the importance of the waterway in the city's growth and prosperity.*

Metropolitan Toronto Reference Library, T-15349

7. CREATING COMMUNITIES

As we have seen in Chapter 6, even before the first ships passed through the Welland Canal on November 30, 1829, settlements had begun at strategic locations along the route: a few shanties for workers here and there, with barns for the horses, sheds for supplies, a few essential services (such as a blacksmith, carpenters, wheelwrights and masons), an office for the contractor or supervisor of works – and, of course, at least one tavern.

As soon as the waterway began to carry its increasing volume of ships and cargoes, it attracted industries, and the primitive "service centres" began to develop into the villages and towns of Port Dalhousie, Merritton, Thorold, Allanburg, Port Robinson, Welland, Dunnville and, by 1833, Port Colborne.

Of all the canal towns, only **St. Catharines** [Fig. 1] had been established before Merritt began his "ditch." In effect, then, the canal *created* the towns along its banks. Even the "Garden City" of St. Catharines owed its transformation from an insignificant rural village to an industrial city to the canals which ran through it [see Chap. 4, Fig. 1]. The Roman Catholic Cathedral [see Chap. 6, Fig. 5] is evidence of the prosperity which the canal had brought to St. Catharines by the 1850s. The Welland Canal Company's office (1855) was located here (overlooking the waterway), and the St. Lawrence Seaway's Western Region headquarters is situated on the west side of the present canal [see Chap. 6, Fig. 21]. The city remains the industrial hub of Niagara.

The canal and its industries helped to make men rich, and they in turn graced the canal communities with beautiful mansions which today, "recycled," continue to serve local people in many practical ways [Fig. 2]. Moreover, in a period when roads were poor, and before the Welland Railway opened in 1859, the canal was the life line between the communities developing along its route.

7.2 St. Catharines, ca. 1980: *"Oak Hill" was built by the canal's founder on Yates Street (named after the American financier J.B. Yates, without whose support the canal might not have been built) in 1860. Oak Hill is now radio station CKTB.*
R.R. Taylor

Attracted by the prospect of work, success and wealth, artisans, professionals and merchants settled in places such as **Port Dalhousie**, the northern terminus of the first three canals. It became a flourishing community, attracting in particular shipbuilding, and ship's suppliers, but also a large rubber mill [Fig. 3]. With the transfer of the canal's northern terminus to Port Weller in 1932, and the end of the Toronto steamship service in 1950, "Port" went into decline, and the town was amalgamated with the expanding St. Catharines in 1960. But in the 1970s a revival began with the refurbishing of "Murphy's" (a former ship chandlery). Other renovations have followed, providing facilities both for local people and the visitors who are now making Port Dalhousie something of a tourist mecca [Fig. 4].

7.3 Port Dalhousie, ca. 1920: *The Third Canal's Lock 1 is at the upper left; to its right, the imposing Consolidated Rubber Factory (formerly Maple Leaf Rubber, established 1900), with Muir Brothers Dry Dock still flourishing next to it.* PAC: PA-30556

7.4 Port Dalhousie, ca. 1980: In 1885 Ed Murphy built a ship chandlery on the site of, first, Johnson's tavern and, in 1877, the Wood House Hotel. Refurbished, "Murphy's" began a movement of restoration that still continues. R.R. Taylor

The newcomers and their families needed homes, schools, churches and a wide range of goods and services. And so the early shantytowns of wooden lean-tos housing immigrant Irish labourers grew into more pretentious villages, with the occasional stone or brick houses and shops. **Merritton**, once "Slabtown" and since 1960 a part of St. Catharines, is another example of the relationship between the waterway, industry, and individual financial success [Fig. 5]. By 1876 it boasted *eight* taverns, catering especially to sailors, canal workers and travellers, and in 1879 it was able to erect a pink Grimsby stone municipal hall [Fig. 6], a proud reminder of boom days.

7.5 Merritton, ca. 1900 (above): *Looking north from the Escarpment, the photographer captured a typical canal townscape of waterways, railways and mills. The Second Canal is in the foreground, with the Riordon Paper Mill. In the middle distance are the trestles of the Welland Railway; the Third Canal is near the horizon.*
SCHM: N-3602

7.6 Merritton, ca. 1980: *The municipal hall (1879) has served at various times as public library, post office, school board office, hydro commission office, police station and community centre. It has been the home of the St. Catharines Historical Museum since 1967.*   R.R. Taylor

At the top of the Niagara Escarpment, **Thorold** (originally "Stumptown") has been a thriving mill town since its beginnings [Figs. 7, 8]. Unlike most of the canal-side communities, it was *not* named after a prominent supporter, but rather after Sir John Thorold, a British M.P. from Lincolnshire. The early saw- and timber mills gave way to the paper industry, after the sulphite process came into general use in the late 1860s, and paper has continued to be a major industry [Fig. 9]. Here, too, canal-based prosperity financed a magnificent home on the hillside overlooking the Second Canal [Fig. 10].

7.7 Thorold, ca. 1882: *The artist's romantic view belies the industrial activity in the town. As early as 1825 Merritt's son had written: "Where the forest stood a short time ago, was now a scene of life and bustle…. One hundred dwellings were on the summit [of the Escarpment], occupied by mechanics, labourers, tailors, shoe-makers, store-keepers and others."*[35] *The stately firehall, built 1878, still stands; the towboys have long since vanished.*   SCHM: N-3674 (*Picturesque Canada*, 1882)

7.8 Thorold, 1919: *Canal townscapes were characterized by factories and mills, usually powered by excess canal water stored in weir ponds behind dams. These wooden mills, with their simple, functional architecture, were still casting their reflections for the photographer to capture.*   PAC: PA-83837

7.9 Thorold, ca. 1928 (above): *Mills still line the Second Canal. Jacob Keefer's Welland Mill, at the far left, is now part of Fraser Paper Mills. The firehall can be seen just across the bridge, permanent by then, since ships no longer passed through the Second Canal. The Third Canal curves through the landscape at the upper right, and the flight locks of the Fourth Canal were under construction (centre). Ontario Paper is off-camera to the lower right.*
PAC: PA-149228

7.10 Thorold, ca. 1980 (left): *George Keefer's son John built this magnificent home, "Maplehurst," on St. David's Road, ca. 1864. It now serves as a nursing home.*
R.R. Taylor

Welland (where the Feeder Canal was connected to the main channel) also has had a history of continued development. First called "Seven Mile Stake," then "Aqueduct" (1829-1842), and then "Merrittsville" (until 1858), it became the county seat for Welland in 1855, testimony to its growing importance. By the 1920s it exhibited a settled affluence, with imposing public and business structures lining Main Street South [Fig. 11], to say nothing of its still surviving Court House [Fig. 12]. Businessmen and residents of the "Rose City" could never forget the presence of the Fourth Canal, as the characteristic lift bridges, necessitated in part by the railways [Fig. 13], dominated the landscape, increasingly disrupting traffic, yet recalling the source of the city's prosperity [Fig. 14].

7.11 Welland, ca. 1920: *From left to right, the Imperial Bank, the Weller Block and the Dominion Building (housing the City Hall, Post Office and Customs House). All overlooked the Third Canal. Only the Weller Block is standing – very much altered.* John Burtniak Coll.

7.12 Welland, ca. 1860: *The city still boasts this handsome Court House, built 1855-62, near the Second Canal, since re-routed.* Tremaine

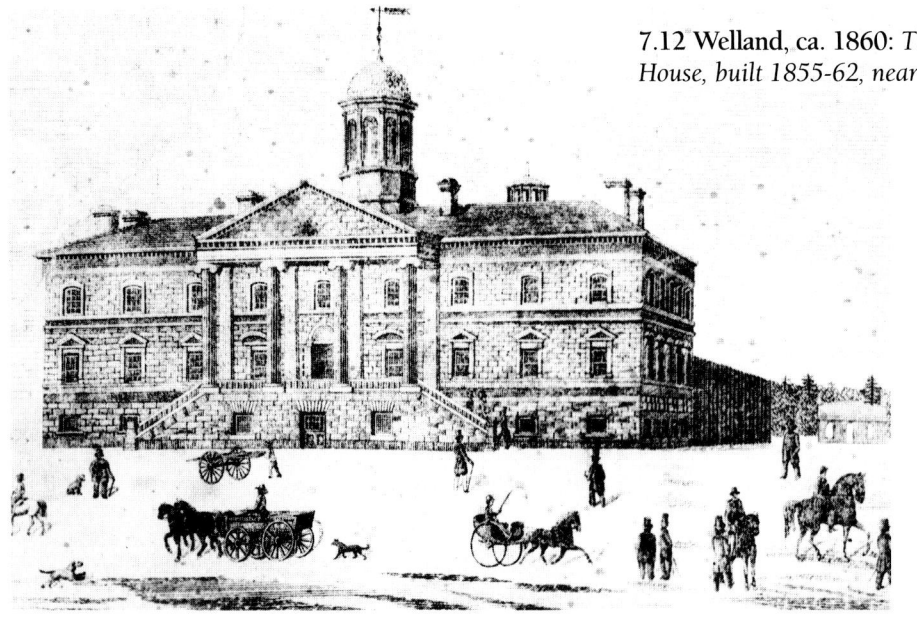

7.13 Welland, 1928: *In 1973 construction of the Welland By-Pass took the ships to the east of the city, allowing cars, trucks and pedestrians to move more freely, and the formerly obstructive bridges were on their way to becoming beloved local landmarks.*
John Burtniak Coll.

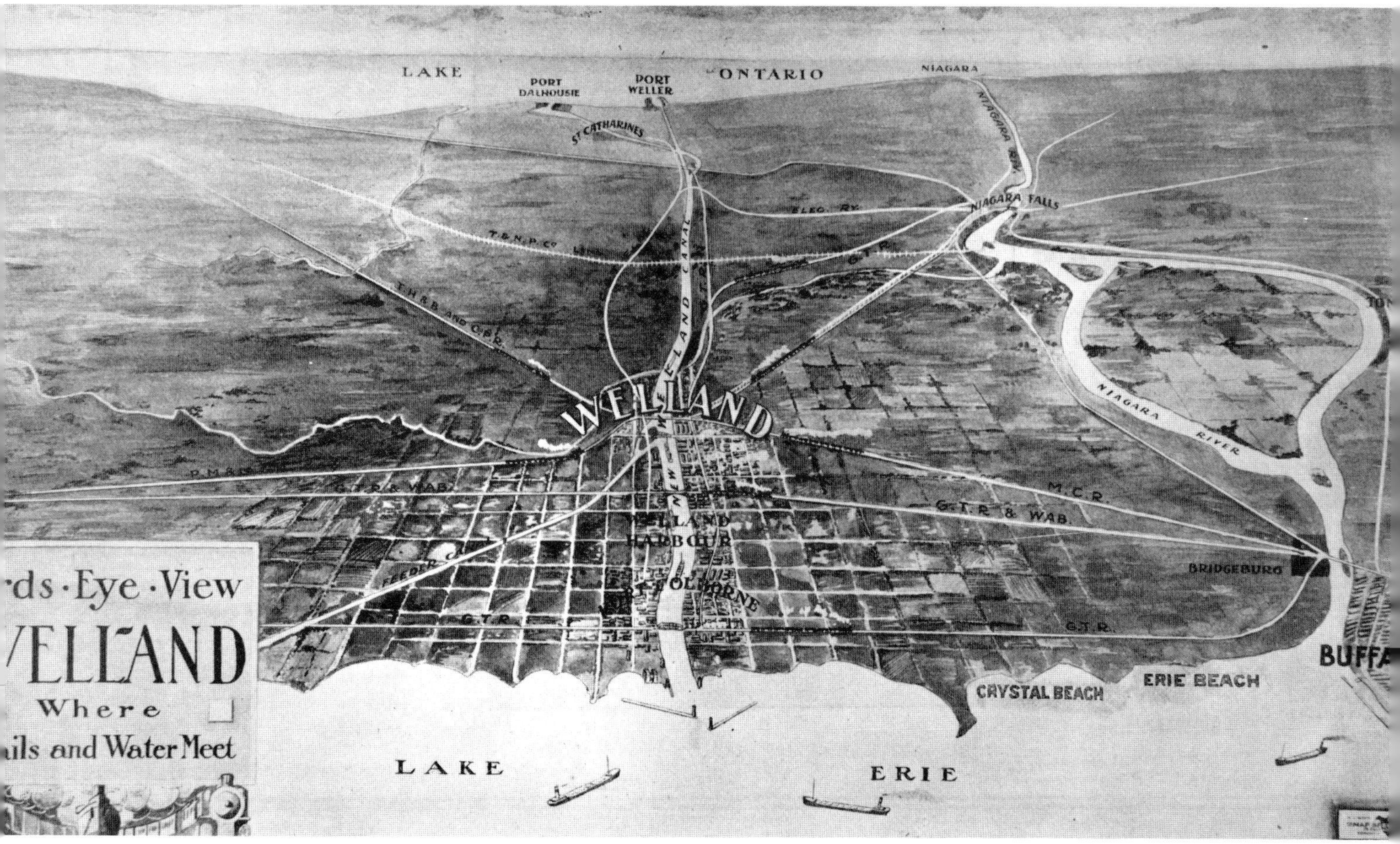

7.14 Welland, ca. 1932: *This view shows Welland proudly at the heart of the Niagara Peninsula. The motto was not unjustified, for here the Feeder Canal joined the Welland River, and the Welland Railway, a link with other towns, passed through. Here, as well, east-west railway lines helped to establish industries and services.* Wellandward

The canal's development, however, could itself bring crisis to a village or town. Deepening of the channel could remove a lock that supplied power for a mill. Widening might displace the "Front Street" running along an earlier channel. A new route might by-pass a settlement that had grown up along an earlier alignment. The canal created towns, but it could also cripple them. For example, because of changes to the canal and its economy, the once thriving settlements of Allanburg and Port Robinson are now only pleasant backwaters.

Allanburg, for instance, "where it all began," flourished for a time [Fig. 15]. It was named after the Honourable William Allan, president of the government-sponsored Bank of Canada and one of the early directors of the Welland Canal Company. Small but successive changes in the canal, widening and deepening, have left little trace of the canal-related industries and businesses [Fig. 16].

7.15 Allanburg, ca. 1890: *As elsewhere, this canal port supplied the necessities of life — and some of its luxuries — to busy workers, sailors, businessmen and visitors. James Upper, proprietor of the Allanburg Hotel in 1865, advertised that his bar was "always well supplied with the best wines, liquours, cigars, &c."* Alfred F. Sagon-King

7.16 Allanburg, ca. 1975: *A cairn among the trees at the near end of the bridge marks the spot where the first sod was turned on November 30, 1824. Today only a few traces of milling activity remain along the Second Canal, visible in the raceway near the junction with the highway (lower right).* Francis Petrie Coll.

Port Robinson, as the terminus of passenger and freight services to Buffalo (along the canal and Feeder to Dunnville), once had numerous hotels, inns and stables catering especially to towboys and their horses. According to Page's *Historical Atlas of the Counties of Lincoln and Welland* (1876) the town had a population of 800-900, and its amenities included schools and churches, two or three taverns, several general stores, some fine mills and two drydocks. Despite this promise, when steam tugs were introduced its function as a port declined. When the port closed in 1890, the population was down to about 400 – just about what it is now [Fig. 17].

Chippawa was the original southern terminus of the Canal, but became independent of it when the Canal was extended from Port Robinson to Lake Erie in 1833. Although no longer a part of the waterway, it should not be forgotten that through this port once passed all Upper Lakes shipping to and from the original Welland Canal [Fig. 18].

7.17 Port Robinson, ca. 1979: Despite the decline, there is still local pride in the town's canal heritage, celebrated annually in "Canal Days" during the summer (see also Afterword). This town, like many others along the canal, was named for one of the canal's influential supporters: the Honourable John Beverley Robinson, Attorney General of Upper Canada.
R.R. Taylor

7.18 Chippawa, ca. 1910: The ERIE BELLE was the last of the sailing vessels to come into Chippawa, and the last to be locked into the Welland Canal at Port Robinson. In the background the Welland River flows into the Niagara. To the right, the man-made Hog Island and the canal channel dug in 1827. John Burtniak Coll.

The Grand River community of **Dunnville** (named after John Henry Dunn, president of the Welland Canal Company until 1833) owed its original prosperity to its location near the Grand River Dam, built to channel river water (needed to raise the level in the main canal) into the Feeder Canal [see Chap. 2]. It became a transshipment port between Lake Erie, the Grand River towns, and the Welland River. In its heyday, shipbuilding was a thriving industry; because of its water power potential, mills were established; and a toll collector and customs officer were stationed here [Figs. 19, 20].

7.19 Dunnville, 1863: *A charming view of a typical canal town in its heyday: bustling and prosperous.*
PAC: C-114134

7.20 Dunnville, ca. 1979: *A pioneer monument (itself an artificial waterfall) celebrates the Grand River Dam. The background of the panel suggests the industry which grew up where the dam created a usable head of water for power. To the best of our knowledge, this is the only monument to falling water!* R.R. Taylor

Unlike Allanburg and Port Robinson, other canal-spawned settlements survived into the 20th century even though the canal had moved away from their hearts. Port Dalhousie, St. Catharines, Thorold and Welland, for instance, no longer straddle the canal, but are still thriving, having gained sufficient momentum through their association with the canal to ensure their continued prosperity. Today, Port Colborne is the only large community created by the canal which maintains its symbiotic relationship.

Twentieth-century **Port Colborne** [Fig. 21] is a far cry from the area described by Mrs. W.H. Merritt in 1833, when the canal was being extended to Lake Erie from Port Robinson: "The ground here is all marsh on both sides of the canal." She also noted that there was "a small ridge with one white house and a store, and some shanties."[36] However, large and small entrepreneurs and businesses were soon attracted, and a bustling port developed. By the 1870s Port Colborne boasted French Second Empire architecture and fashionable shops: the latest in building styles and the dry goods imported [Fig. 22].

The growth of Port Colborne, like that of St. Catharines, has included the disappearance of an earlier community, **Humberstone**, also known for a time as "Petersburg" [Fig. 23]. In the latter years of the 19th century it was a flourishing village, with (among other industries) a cutlery and flatware manufactory referred to as "the largest in Canada." Among the canal communities, Humberstone was distinguished by the presence of a Lutheran church.

By the 1930s Port Colborne was well on its way to becoming a sophisticated harbour with a large anchorage area, many service quays, wharves for winter berthage, and a modern industrial complex. The two large grain elevators on Lake Erie document the city's role (then as now) as a vital transshipment centre for grain [Fig. 24; see also Chap. 4, Fig. 20].

7.21 Port Colborne, ca. 1920: *From the west, the Lake Erie terminus of the canal flanks two locks: the closer one, a Second Canal lift lock; the farther, a Third Canal guard lock. East and West Streets paralleled the length of the old stone structures, while swing bridges carried rail and road traffic over the canal.*
John Burtniak Coll.

7.22 Port Colborne, ca. 1885: *Carter's store, which also housed the local Post Office, still stands.*
AO: Acc. 13967-20

7.23 Humberstone, ca. 1920: *"Waiting for the bridge." Still flourishing in the 1920s, Humberstone was absorbed into Port Colborne in 1952.* John Burtniak Coll.

Like many other Niagara Peninsula communities, Port Colborne has felt the effects of economic changes in the 1970s and 1980s. But one fact has not changed: the names of canal towns bear witness still to the great era of canal-building, from 1824 to 1833. They recall the men associated directly or indirectly with the waterway's inception and growth; they often remind us of those pioneers' British ancestry, and they suggest the canal-builders' desire to honour the men in power who encouraged and protected the audacious enterprise.

In all, nine settlements were created because of the canal and its requirements. They were located on the waterway's banks and grew as the canal itself prospered and grew. Our pictures show them at various stages of their development, with their canal-related industries and businesses, drydocks, wharves, locks, weir ponds and general bustle. Even before 1900 they had become living monuments to the ambition and energy of the thousands who had flocked here – and stayed – to work and dwell on or near Merritt's canal.

7.24 Port Colborne, ca. 1930: *Widening of the canal channel for the Fourth Canal eliminated the small swing bridges [see Chap. 10, Fig. 11] and replaced them with the two lift bridges (numbers 20 and 21), which carry Highway 3 and the Canadian National Railway over the present canal. At the lower right can be seen locks of both the Second and Third Canals.* PAC: PA-48202

8.1 Lock 12, Third Canal, 1880s: *If the artist C.J. Dyer is to be believed, well-to-do gentlemen took their fashionable ladies for sociable strolls through at least some of the building sites of the Third Canal. Here the "smart set" — with bustles, parasols and canes — examine an unfinished lock, the gates of which are not yet in place. However, the wooden floor and the very fine stonework were much admired.* Can. Illust. News, 1876, p. 44

8. PEOPLE AND PLEASURES

Throughout its history the Welland Canal has attracted admirers, the curious and well-wishers. As already noted, Sir Peregrine Maitland, when Lieutenant-Governor of Upper Canada, was a frequent visitor, bringing friends along. Another visitor was William Hamilton Merritt's wife – obviously an interested party. Late in March of 1829, for example, she was one of a sleighing party that went from St. Catharines to the Grand River:

> Proceeding by the Deep Cut seven miles up to the Chippewa [Welland River], where they found the piers sunk for the aqueduct, and then travelling four or five miles through a thinly settled country to Marshville [later Wainfleet]....This place was the headquarters of the Engineer on the Feeder. After dining, they proceeded in a straight course for ten miles through the marsh, passing occasionally a few shanties, where people were at work digging....She [Mrs. Merritt] expresses surprise at the healthiness of the people, and associates it with the fact of the water being impregnated with tamarac.[37]

In 1841 a local farmer told a visitor that the Welland Canal was "far better worth...[wasting] time on than the Falls of Niagara...."[38] Thousands since have agreed with him, not only because of its fascinating locks and exotic ships, but also because of the opportunities for leisure associated with being on, in, or near the water [Figs. 1, 2].

8.2 "And All I Ask is a Tall Ship:" *In 1975 this replica of the original Canadian racing schooner, the BLUENOSE, recalled the first ships ever to ply the waterway. Note the Homer Bridge, up for the vessel's passage, with the Garden City Skyway in the background – other than a tunnel, the only really satisfactory solution to the conflict between land and water traffic [see Chap. 10, Fig. 15].*

St. Lawrence Seaway Authority: Western Region

Generations of ship-watchers attest to this. "As I look from my window," wrote a St. Catharines resident in 1853, "I see among the forest trees...the masts and riggings of large vessels, moving slowly along. A bend in the canal hides the water from sight and the only objects visible are the stationary trees and the moving vessels."[39] A century and a half later, the same experience is a common phenomenon, and one of the reasons why ship-watching has been a popular pastime for both Niagara residents and visitors. Tourists and locals alike are delightfully astonished by the spectacle of a sea-going freighter, wearing the flag of some distant country, apparently sailing through meadows, orchards or residential suburbs [Fig. 3].

The flight of twinned locks in Thorold, where ships climb or descend the Escarpment, is a major vantage point, a spot probably unexcelled anywhere else in the world [Fig. 4]. Here and elsewhere the curious may view some unusual vessel passing by: a battleship [Fig. 5], a replica of an historic ship [Fig. 6], the occasional surviving sailing vessel [Fig. 2], or the royal yacht [Fig. 7]. Identifying, photographing, drawing or painting the different kinds of ships is a hobby for many. Blasts from ships' whistles punctuate the days and nights of people who rarely see even the nearest of the Great Lakes. Here, in the continent's heart, home ports and cargo types are subjects of lively discussion as vessels from around the world pass our front doors.

8.3 Near the Garden City Skyway, ca. 1975: *Popular sights for ship-watchers are the "salties," the ocean-going vessels. "Now...is Bergen in Sweden or Norway?...Have we seen that smokestack symbol before?...What is she carrying?...How do you know?"* Barry Schneider

8.5 Welland, 1980 (opposite, middle): *HMCS NIPIGON, passing through the canal, was a reminder that the original canal was built in the wake of the War of 1812, and in fear of American expansion and aggression. Hundreds turned out to watch or visit the warship on its friendly tour.* Alfred F. Sagon-King

8.6 Lock 1, Port Dalhousie, 1893 (opposite, bottom): *Re-creations of bygone sailing ships are not solely a 20th-century phenomenon. In 1893 replicas of Christopher Columbus' three vessels used the waterway to reach the Chicago World's Fair. The SANTA MARIA was built in Spain with American funds to celebrate the 400th anniversary of Columbus' voyage. She was 75 feet (almost 23 m) long, with a beam of 27 feet (8.2 m) and a displacement of 127 tons.* SCHM: N-2118

8.4 Lock 7, Thorold, ca. 1985: *The original part of the Lock Seven Motel (the boxlike white building, centre top) was built as a residence for Fourth Canal construction engineers. It has become a well-established tradition that visiting canal buffs should stay there, since the amenities include unparalleled opportunities for ship-watching and the lobby has a receiver for ship-to-shore radio calls. Vessels such as the ALGOWAY can be viewed not only from the vantage point of the motel's balconies, but even, as some buffs know well, from their beds!*   Lock Seven Motel

8.7 Royal Visitors, 1959: *When Queen Elizabeth II came to North America to open the St. Lawrence Seaway, she and Prince Philip sailed through the Welland Canal in the sleek and luxurious yacht BRITANNIA. Admiring crowds gathered at strategic viewing points to welcome the royal visitors.* Alfred F. Sagon-King

8.8 "In the Good Old Summertime," 1910: *What better day's holiday than to take the DALHOUSIE CITY from the Welland Vale wharf near St. Catharines, sail down Twelve Mile Creek, across Martindale Pond, through Lock 1 (Third Canal), and, picking up passengers at Port Dalhousie, set out for Toronto across cool, breezy Lake Ontario?* John Burtniak Coll.

The man-made harbours, ponds and parks along the canals have long attracted holiday-makers. For half a century after the service began in 1901, fun-seekers arrived in Port Dalhousie on steamers from Toronto to "make a day of it." Many Torontonian "day-trippers" can still recall the sinking feeling they had when they missed the last boat home! [Figs. 8, 9] Upon disembarking in "Port" they might go on to St. Catharines and the Falls (on the Niagara, St. Catharines and Toronto Railway), or stay at Lakeside Park in Port Dalhousie (developed after 1902) to enjoy the beach, the swimming, the rides and games, or to watch the ships or the annual regatta [Figs. 10-12]. (The famous 1892 carousel, with its painted animals and 1867 organ, has been restored and is once again in operation.)

8.9 **Port Dalhousie, ca. 1905:** *The GARDEN CITY, from Toronto, is about to leave. On the left, cars of the Niagara, St. Catharines and Toronto Railway await passengers for a return trip to Niagara Falls. The terminus of the Welland Railway is across the harbour; Lakeside Park is just out of sight at the left.* SCHM: N-1544

8.10 **Port Dalhousie, 1920s:** *Enjoying Lakeside Park, built on land reclaimed from the mouth of the Twelve Mile Creek by the canal-builders.* SCHM: N-3839

The Royal Canadian Henley Regatta has been held in Port Dalhousie ever since 1903, when the Canadian Association of Amateur Oarsmen began holding their annual championships on Martindale Pond. In 1904 a grandstand and shellhouse were built at the south end of the course; a new grandstand was constructed in 1931 [Fig. 13].

8.11 Port Dalhousie, ca. 1930: *The waterslide at Lakeside Park was a great attraction, but obviously the adjacent beach, the canal piers, the terminus of the Toronto steamers, and the railway to Niagara Falls offered something for every taste.* John Burtniak Coll.

8.12 Port Dalhousie, 1960: *At the annual Royal Canadian Henley Regatta on Martindale Pond (created by the second and third canal weirs), six crews vie for first place. The excitement and skill of the race has drawn participants and audiences to the scene since 1903. One of the last ships to moor in the inner harbour can be seen at upper right.* SCHM: N-1688

One can still fish or canoe on Martindale Pond [Fig. 14], or have a refreshing picnic along its tree-lined shores. After 1950, when the steamer service stopped (because of competition from the Queen Elizabeth Way), Lakeside Park itself declined; however, in the 1970s it began to revive. Today the whole of Port Dalhousie is again attracting both out-of-towners and locals to its restored restaurants and shops, and to its special atmosphere born of the town's canal heyday [see Chap. 7, Figs. 3, 4].

8.13 **Port Dalhousie, ca. 1910:** *Across from the Henley grandstand these spectators might be waiting for, or watching, boat or swimming races, log rolling, or target practice — or just enjoying the music of a floating band. Umbrellas and wide-brimmed hats kept off the hot August sun!*   John Burtniak Coll.

8.14 **Port Dalhousie, 1910:** *The Henley also provided an opportunity for canoeing — and courting. This couple has probably taken a close look at a racing scull (background right) near the typical Third Canal swing bridge.*   SCHM: N-1768

In fact, the whole length of the canal system has always offered attractive spots for recreation. At the turn of the century, for example, the banks of the Third Canal were often dotted with summertime picnickers and fishermen [Fig. 15], while hardier types rode on horseback along the towpaths. Canoeists found stretches of placid water ideal for leisurely trips or for races; fishermen still find challenge in quieter sections of abandoned weirs and ponds. While swimming [Fig. 16] has been forbidden in the Fourth Canal, it remains a summertime ritual in abandoned stretches of the earlier waterways.

8.15 Merritton, 1875 (left): *Summer pleasures included fishing, of course! These two fishermen try their luck in the Second Canal, not far from Lock 7 and the Phelps brothers' mill. On the hill is Noah Phelps' home, which still stands.* Page's Atlas

8.16 Port Colborne, ca. 1890 (below): *At the south end of the canal the breakwater protected a quiet beach, providing wading and other genteel bathing pleasures for the fashionably dressed. (The gentleman wearing a hat is the lighthouse keeper, David Fortier.)* PCHMM

In winter months, skating and hockey [Fig. 17] on the canal were once more popular (and possible) than today. At Allanburg, for instance, four inches (over 10 cm) of ice – which could hold a team of horses – was considered the safe thickness for individual skaters or for iceboats. Empty locks of the Third Canal were used for lacrosse games. But the frozen waters of the canals provided profit as well as fun, whether in the form of fish [Fig. 18] or ice to fill the area's ice-boxes before refrigerators became common [see Chap. 4, Fig. 18].

8.17 Near St. Catharines, 1920s: *Skaters of all ages and hockey players (centre) enjoy the Third Canal. Today, most of the lower portion (from Thorold) of the present canal is drained in the winter, so skating is no longer possible, except on the abandoned stretch through Welland.*   SCHM: N-3608

8.18 Welland, 1982: *Hardy types fish through the ice for smelt or perch when the water of the abandoned section of the Third Canal freezes over!*   J.N. Jackson

Pleasure cruises on and through the waterway were also more frequent in the past: until not too long ago, lake cruisers regularly plied the canals [Figs. 19, 20; also Figs. 8, 9]. Although these services have ended, Niagara College has recently begun to offer a day-long cruise on the operating canal each spring. And among the lakers and salties, jaunty cabin cruisers can still be seen making their way through the present canal.

8.19 and 20 Port Colborne, ca. 1900: *While the northern terminus drew pleasure-seekers from Toronto, the southern terminus also attracted crowds. This group, probably from a Buffalo steamer, poses at Cronmiller and White's brewery. Judging by the lapel ribbons, they all belong to some club or organization. Their excursion no doubt included ship-watching and time on the beach, as well as testing the local products! Late in the afternoon they rejoin their festively flagged ship for the return cruise after a fun-filled day which might have included a visit to Erie Park, on the east side of the canal.* PCHMM

Speaking of ships, "firsts" have always lured crowds to the canal's banks, as in 1829 when the ANNIE AND JANE and the R.H. BROUGHTON made their inaugural journeys through Merritt's "ditch" [see Introd., Fig. 1]; or in 1932, when the LEMOYNE opened the Fourth Canal [see Chap. 5, Fig. 11]. The passage of especially interesting vessels, such as a captured German submarine, has also attracted notice [Fig. 21]. In fact, during World War II (1939-1945) barbed wire fences and barricades had to be used to keep the curious public away from the canal—particularly crucial then to national defence.

8.21 Third Canal, 1919: *One of the most unusual sights ever seen on the Welland Canal was this captured German submarine, UC-97, booty from World War I.*
SCHM: N-6165

8.22 Port Colborne, ca. 1910: *Bunting-bedecked yachts line the west side of the harbour, waiting for their owners to take them out on Gravelly Bay and Lake Erie. In the meantime, the canal harbour provides a safe haven.* John Burtniak Coll.

The canals are now a focus of ever-increasing leisure activity. Even small centres such as Allanburg offer a cairn for history buffs (at the site of the turning of the first sod in 1824), picnic tables at canal-side, a baseball diamond, and, for canal enthusiasts, tantalizing remnants of three canals, while the local lift bridge in operation never fails to fascinate [see Chap. 10, Fig. 21]. Larger communities can offer more: for example, Port Colborne has a viewing hill (with fountain and garden) at Lock 8; a grassy promenade on old West Street near the canal mouth; and a large park with marina and boat launch, protected by the harbour breakwater, at Gravelly Bay [Fig. 22]. Fishing is good here as well, in the abandoned channel of the Third Canal. Nearby, what was a canal-created swamp (Mud Lake) is now a provincial wildlife management area [see Chap.10, Fig. 2]. At Welland, the stretch of the Fourth Canal rendered redundant by construction of the By-Pass is now used for water-skiing, canoeing and swimming, while its banks are being developed for picnic sites. The Second Canal aqueduct functioned as a public swimming pool from 1946 until 1984. Nearby, the area where the Welland River leaves the syphon culvert offers sport for fishermen.

At Thorold the twin flight locks of the Fourth Canal are as compelling an attraction now as they were when opened, 50 years ago [see Frontispiece]. Nearby, along the Second Canal route, the city built the Battle of Beaverdams Park to commemorate both an incident in the War of 1812 and its canal heritage. In St. Catharines, the Lock 3 observation platform is usually thronged in the summer, while the Merritt Trail (see Afterword, Fig. 3) encourages those with more time to take a nostalgic walk or ride along the abandoned Second Canal. St. Catharines, Port Colborne, and other communities, hold annual "Canal Days" featuring museum displays, ship models, naval shows, local crafts and good things to eat.

8.23 North of St. Catharines, ca. 1905: *From its inception the Welland Canal has fascinated visitors and locals alike. The boy lounging in the doorway of the lockmaster's office at Lock 4 (Third Canal) is typical. What sort of ship, from what exotic place, did he watch? What were his dreams... his future? Unhappily, today only one of these charming offices, with their shutters and "gingerbread," remains: a delightful reminder of a type of structure which at one time contributed to the unique character of the Niagara peninsula landscape.*
OA: Murphy Collection (5)

When he conceived of the canal, Merritt was not thinking of casually clad tourists with their instamatic cameras and sunburn, nor of local people seeking relaxation on their days off. Nevertheless, he created for both not only the livelihood to allow for leisure, but also a source of inexpensive yet priceless recreation [Figs. 23-25; and see Afterword]. But both work and pleasure could be overshadowed by catastrophe, and prosperity would not always continue, as the following chapter will show.

8.24 On the Old Feeder Canal, ca. 1910.   John Burtniak Coll.

8.25 "Canal Rats" at Welland, ca. 1920.   Welland Historical Museum

9.1 Thorold, 1928: *At Lock 6, a crane carrying an end post for the 500-ton steel gate collapsed on 1 August 1928, killing ten men and injuring 20 others.*
Alfred F. Sagon-King

9.2 Expendable: *A tombstone in the Victoria Lawn Cemetery in St. Catharines commemorates two workers killed in the construction accident at Lock 6: a rare memorial.* R.R. Taylor

9. DIFFICULTIES AND DISASTERS

Building and rebuilding the Welland Canals has created communities, industries and jobs, and provided opportunities for recreation – but not without cost. Construction, maintenance and repairs have been difficult and expensive, both in terms of money and in suffering – both human and animal – including loss of life. The elegant visitors shown visiting a Third Canal lock [Chap. 8, Fig. 1] probably neither knew nor cared about such fatalities as occurred during construction accidents.

Moreover, defending the canals against a perceived foreign threat posed a challenge in the 19th century, and even as late as the First World War (1914-1918). No review of the waterway's history would be complete, or truthful, if it neglected the difficulties which the canals have created or the disasters which occasionally have occurred on, or because of, them [Fig. 1].

Building the waterways was fraught with problems from the beginning, as we have already seen (Chap. 2). The climate, labour problems and disease helped to exacerbate serious financial difficulties. For workers, making a living on construction could be a fatal undertaking, for not only were cholera and malaria rampant (in the early days), but accidents on the building sites regularly took their toll. In May 1844, during the building of the flight locks near Merritton, a man was crushed to death and another injured when a large stone, being lifted by a crane, fell on them. Nor were supervisors immune from danger. In 1826, for example, a contractor, James Dwyer, was fatally injured on a construction site. The work of improving the canals has also led to tragedies, as in 1876, when a worker using nitroglycerine in the blasting to deepen the harbour at Port Colborne was blown to bits.

While increasing sophistication of machinery and more stringent safety measures may have decreased the percentage of accidents per number of workers involved, injuries and fatalities have not been eliminated. In 1926 men working on the then new Fourth Canal were crushed when a massive concrete slab fell on them. Another fatal accident occurred two years later [Fig. 1] and was vividly recalled by a worker:

> I was running a gasoline locomotive hauling concrete in there. There were two cranes.... Well, this one here was clamped to the tracks, stationary; it couldn't move. And the one here, it was allowed to move. So they picked up a beam and that one held it on the one end, and this one here was allowed to move so they could straighten it. Picked it up and turned it. He came along here, and he got right behind the gate and this one was right at the gate. Why, the cable on the crane that was stationary broke! Well, there was nothing to hold the other one from going over. This big beam, you know, was too much for one crane. She went over, she went down behind the gate and pushed the gate over on the other one. And oh! it just cut men in two and everything. There was men working on the inside of the gate when it happened. Ah! it was a mess![40]

On projects of such magnitude, said Alexander Grant, Chief Engineer of the Fourth Canal, one could expect one man's death per one million dollars expenditure. The Fourth Canal cost $130 million; 118 men died on the sites from 1912 to 1932 [Fig. 2].

In the early years, not all communities in the Niagara Peninsula welcomed the canals. Nor did all profit from them. The citizens of Niagara-on-the-Lake were dismayed when their town did not become the northern terminus of the original canal. In addition, "There were many dissatisfied at having the canal pass through their farms," as J.P. Merritt wrote about local residents in 1826, "and they held a meeting at Beaverdams, favouring the route by the Twenty Mile Creek, Niagara, or any other place but that along the 'Twelve'."[41] Other villages or towns — St. Johns, for example — originally prosperous, dwindled and even vanished when the waterway drew trade away from their mills and businesses [Fig. 3]. In short, canal construction has created difficulties both for individuals [Fig. 4] and for communities, some of which lost local recreational areas [Fig. 5] or business streets [Fig. 6]. Other communities have disappeared [Fig. 7], or seen their promise of prosperity remain unfulfilled [Fig. 8].

9.3 St. Johns, ca. 1862: *Before the First Welland Canal was built, St. Johns (on Twelve Mile Creek) was the industrial heart of Upper Canada. Still a thriving village as late as 1862, its woollen factory, iron foundry and other water-powered mills slowly declined in the later 19th century as entrepreneurs moved to the canal's banks. Today there is scarcely a trace remaining of this pioneer community.* St. Johns Outdoor Studies Centre

9.4 Disappearing Farm Land, 1914: *Those opposed to the route of the First Canal would have sympathized with the farmer whose barn tottered on the edge of the Fourth Canal's channel!* SCHM: N-1318

9.5 McCalla's Park, ca. 1910: *A charming recreational area was lost when this section of Ten Mile Creek (at what is now Port Weller) was devoured for construction of Lock 1 of the Fourth Canal.*
SCHM: N-2896

9.6 Port Colborne, ca. 1910: *These government buildings and business premises were demolished when Fourth Canal construction swallowed up East Street. Third Canal locks in the foreground, however, have survived to this day.* John Burtniak Coll.

9.7 Homer, 1980: *In 1876 Homer, a village on Ten Mile Creek, situated on the Queenston Road (now Highway 8), three miles east of St. Catharines, boasted a population of 200. In 1913 it stood in the way of the Fourth Canal; today, only the cemetery and a few unrelated buildings mark its site.* R.R. Taylor

9.8 Port Weller, 1932: *The Fourth Canal's large new harbour on Lake Ontario created what seemed to be an ideal site for a future industrial community, as this scene suggests. But when the Great Depression intervened, the hoped for development never materialized, as later industry was attracted to pre-existing canal communities. Today the area is part of St. Catharines.* SCHM: N-1822

The passage of ships through the locks has not been without fatal accidents, even in our presumably more safety-conscious times [Figs. 9, 10]. In 1975 a Seaway worker was killed at Lock 6 when a mooring cable on a ship gave way; and in 1980 a seaman trying to jump aboard his ship fell into Lock 7 and drowned. When Bridge 12 in Port Robinson was rammed by the ore carrier STEELTON in 1974, one man was killed, the weather station was destroyed, and 50 vessels were detained for two weeks as cranes worked to remove the debris. In addition, the little community was permanently divided [Fig. 11].

9.9 Near Thorold, 1912: *A mechanical breakdown in its engine room sent the government steamship LA CANADIENNE smashing through the gates of Lock 22 of the Third Canal. The resulting small tidal wave drowned three boys who were fishing in the reach beyond the lock.*   SCHM: N-2211

9.10 Allanburg, 1966: *After the STONEFAX collided with the ARTHUR STOVE, she spent six weeks on the bottom of the canal. Although such collisions do not always take human lives, they frequently disrupt traffic and cause considerable loss to shipowners, merchants, and the Seaway and port authorities.*   Alfred F. Sagon-King

9.11 Port Robinson, ca. 1979: *Following the loss of the lift bridge which had united the village, a tiny passenger ferry connects its severed sections. But the community's decline was noticeable much earlier: in 1876 the population was over 800; by 1885 it had dropped to about 400. In the era of the Third Canal, ship design changed, undercutting the town's main industry, the construction of wooden ships.*
Alfred F. Sagon-King

Even more recently, and of much more widespread impact, was the collapse of a 150-foot (45.7 m) section of the 53-year-old concrete wall of Lock 7 in Thorold, in October 1985 [Fig. 12]. The Liberian grain freighter FURIA was trapped against the opposite wall, and while nobody was injured, it was feared that the entire lock might cave in. Fortunately, it did not. But the necessary repairs (which took over three weeks) halted traffic, resulting in curtailment of grain shipments and severe loss to shipping companies, and "caused a panic in Rotterdam when a cargo of

9.12 Thorold, October, 1985: *Near disaster in Lock 7.*   Canapress Photo Service

Canadian flaxseed failed to arrive in time."[42] When the canal re-opened, more than 125 ships were lined up awaiting passage, including 50 downbound with cargoes of grain for export. Officials estimated that the accident would cost about $50 million in lost revenue and operating costs, since traffic along the St. Lawrence Seaway was paralyzed at the busiest time of year, when vessels were racing to finish their trips before the winter closing of the Welland Canal.

For over a century and a half, a major threat to the efficiency of the canals has been not so much mechanical breakdown as their own vital resource: water. For instance, the wash of passing ships damaged the canal banks, causing erosion and slumping. This was especially a problem for the First Canal, as it was built too economically (see Chap. 2). The mills, which depended on the canal for their waterpower, could in turn create problems for passing ships, since the large amounts of water drawn into the mill wheels could cause a strong current, sucking ships off course. And the volume of water they required could significantly lower the water level, affecting both ships and other mill-owners. The aqueducts of the first two canals near Welland created problems: the first one leaked badly, while the second proved dangerous to ships, since the water levels in it varied from time to time, and ships' captains often had to wait for favourable winds to bring more water into the system from Lake Erie before they could cross the structure. In its frozen form, too, water could cause problems, as when in 1826 ice filled the large elevated raceway from Merritton to St. Catharines [Fig. 13], causing it to collapse. In its early days, until the channel was deepened in 1842, the Feeder Canal from Dunnville would frequently become blocked by grass (in the marshy section), interrupting navigation. Flooding, too, could cause disruption [Fig. 14].

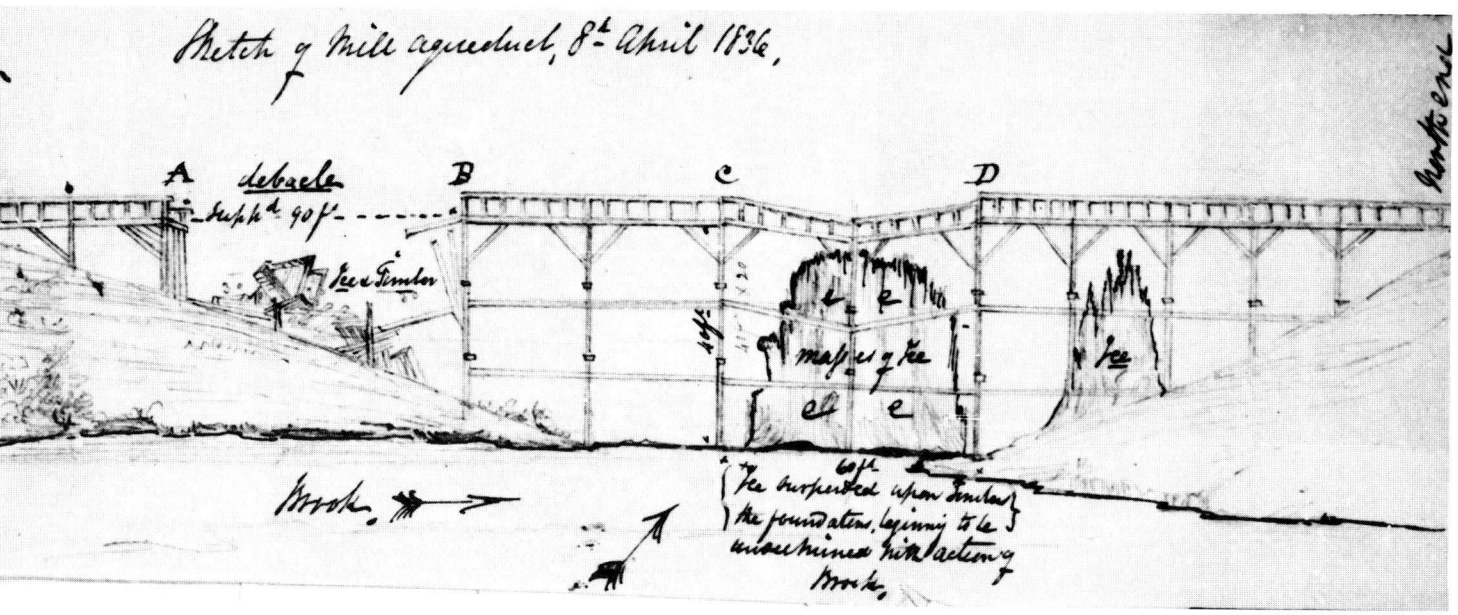

9.13 St. Catharines, 1836: *The forces of nature could create problems. For example, melting ice, floating in great chunks, jammed up and caused the collapse of parts of the Merritton – St. Catharines raceway in the spring of 1836 (a disaster equivalent to a massive hydro-electric blackout or the stoppage of oil supplies today).*
AO: Merritt Papers, Package 13, MS-74(2)

The very men who benefitted from the waterpower provided by the canal in turn caused damage to their source of prosperity. Mention has already been made of the strong currents and lowered water levels caused by the mills, which also were responsible for polluting the waters (not only a 20th-century phenomenon!). As early as 1836 sawmill owners were reprimanded for dumping sawdust into the canal waters, where it formed bars hazardous to ships. Paper mills *still* pollute the water of the Second Canal where it flows from Thorold north through St. Catharines [Fig. 15].

9.14 Dunnville, 1913: *The water which the canal-builders used to help create their masterpiece, and which helped to create prosperous towns, could also threaten the viability of both communities and waterway. Here, the Grand River has flooded Canal Street so that it resembles its namesake!* John Burtniak Coll.

9.15 Mountain Locks Park, St. Catharines, 1971: *The historic "Neptune's Staircase" [see Chap. 2, Fig. 1] is befouled by effluent from a local paper mill. Earlier forms of pollution were directly detrimental to the industrial economy; today such pollution prevents the development of this area as a recreational and educational resource. The still sturdy and beautifully crafted stonework of the 150-year-old locks is a compelling reason for considering them historic monuments.*
Alfred F. Sagon-King

WELLAND CANAL.

WARNING NOTICE TO LOCKTENDERS.

A serious accident and injury to the foot gates of Lock 10 having recently occurred through the gross negligence of Assistant Lockmaster Hare, he has in consequence been suspended. The damage in the present case was caused by the water being hoisted at the head gates before first seeing that the foot gates were properly mitred.

I have reason to believe this dangerous practice has been by no means unusual on other Locks.

This caution notice is now issued for all Locktenders' guidance in future, because immediate dismissal will follow in every case where similar neglect occurs.

WILLIAM ELLIS,
Superintendent.

Welland Canal Office,
May 10th, 1888.

9.16 St. Catharines, 1888.   SCHM

Whether simple or sophisticated, machinery works only as well as its human operators. Ships, locomotives, bridges, lock gates and construction equipment, all require alert and careful handling if catastrophe is to be avoided [Fig. 16]. Human error has led to numerous and varied accidents, as ships have sunk in the canals, rammed the bridges, or failed to stop when entering locks. The first serious example of the latter sort of mishap occurred in 1833, when a schooner crashed through four gates at Lock 2. Since the coming of the railways, their bridges have been the scene of derailments, resulting in blockage of the waterway by locomotives and cars, as well as damage to the bridges themselves [Fig. 17].

9.17 Near Welland, 1876: *Human negligence caused this accident and the death of the driver of the locomotive, who had ignored a red stoplight. But perhaps he had not known that this swing bridge, which crossed the canal near Welland, was always left open to facilitate growing canal traffic. The locomotive (of a Canada Southern Railway eastbound freight) sank completely into the canal, and 11 boxcars were ripped to splinters.*   DeVolpi (Can. Illust. News, 1876)

Human malice has also endangered the canal — a natural target for foreign saboteurs because of its value to the economy and defence of Canada. The greatest damage to the waterway from human violence occurred in 1841, when one of the Allanburg locks was blown up by Fenian sympathizers. Then, during the Fenian invasions of the 1860s, a special military battery was created to defend the canal [Fig. 18]. The Fenians were active again in 1900, when a group from New York State dynamited Lock 24 at Thorold. The lock gates were blown apart for a few seconds, after which the pressure of water closed them, much to the disappointment of the plotters [Fig. 19], who had hoped to cause a mile-long flood below the Escarpment. Consequently, during World War I, soldiers patrolled the length of the waterway [Fig. 20].

Even people not associated in any way with the canal could suffer. For example, the opening of the First Canal in 1829 allowed parasitic lampreys to move from Lake Erie to Lake Ontario. Until the 1960s, when chemical measures provided some control, the lampreys destroyed fish and threatened the livelihood of fishermen — as they are once again beginning to do. Deepening of the canal near Allanburg in 1957 led to wells drying up, and the blasting caused plaster ceilings to fall in on the heads of residents in the area. In the 1970s expropriation of land on the east bank, for a new canal, was deemed an unnecessary hardship by those who lost their homes and farmlands.

9.18 Near Port Colborne, 1865: *During the American Civil War local residents, worried about the exposed position of the vital waterway, formed the Welland Canal Field Battery to defend the canal. They feared possible attack from the Northern States, seeking to weaken Britain's support of the Southern Confederacy. Equipped with two large guns (the other was at Port Robinson), they defended the canal against the Fenian invaders who attacked in 1866.* DeVolpi (Can. Illust. News, 1879)

9.19 The Saboteurs of 1900 (inset): *John Walsh, John Nolan and Karl Dullman (alias Luke Dillan) were arrested, tried and imprisoned for their crime. They were probably protesting against British rule in Ireland, but there is speculation that they may have been linked with grain handlers in Buffalo who, if traffic was disrupted on the Welland, would have benefitted from the resulting forced unloading of ships in the American port.* Francis Petrie Coll.

9.20 Along the Welland, ca. 1916: *During the First World War (1914-18) fear of Fenian invasions led to formation of four units of the Lincoln and Welland, and the Wentworth Regiments to guard the waterway. After America entered the war in 1917, the need for defence diminished, but by that time the "Welland Canal Force" had grown to more than 1,000 men. Meanwhile, vessels were regularly boarded and searched, and noone was allowed to disembark in transit.* PAC: PA-5127

It is a common saying that every great enterprise is worth effort and sacrifice. We may tend to forget that the Welland Canals were a "great enterprise" – and as such have occasioned much human drama and personal tragedy. At the official opening of the Fourth Canal in 1932, the Minister of Railways and Canals, the Hon. Dr. R.J. Manion, said:

> In due course, we shall see that the names of these workmen [killed during construction] are suitably preserved and made an enduring portion of the great structure that rises as a monument not only to their effort and their lives, but to the efforts of thousands of working men and engineering helpers whose unremitting toil, often in the face of difficulty and discouragement, made possible the triumph of this hour.[43]

As yet, there are no such monuments, plaques or signs along the Welland Canals: only the canal itself, and the changes it wrought on the landscape of the Niagara Peninsula.

10.1 North of Thorold, ca. 1919 (above): *As it approaches the Niagara Escarpment, the Third Canal looks like a giant, man-made river. The descending tons of water are channelled and controlled by human devices — locks, weirs and ponds.* John Burtniak Coll.

10.2 Mud Lake Wildlife Management Area, 1982 (left): *Spoil dumped during construction of the Fourth Canal created, over decades, a new marsh just north of Port Colborne. The marsh attracted wildlife, and recently imaginative conservationists have protected the area, creating a boardwalk, trails, and hunting and observation blinds.* R.R. Taylor

10. TRANSFORMING THE LANDSCAPE

The builders of the First Welland Canal audaciously created a new "river" running north through the whole Niagara Peninsula [see Chap. 1, Fig. 9; Chap. 2, Fig. 16]. Since then, on an ever-increasing scale, the Welland Canals have further transformed the local landscape, a process which seems likely to continue long into the future.

The original builders "canalized" Twelve Mile Creek from St. Catharines to Port Dalhousie, as well as the portion of Dick's Creek which ran through St. Catharines [see Chap. 4, Fig. 1]. Successive rebuildings of the canals have created a network of criss-crossing waterways and ponds [Fig. 1]. In particular, the second and third canals formed huge weirs, as well as smaller "rivers" – the raceway in St. Catharines and the Feeder Canal. And the builders of the Fourth Canal transformed the course of the Ten Mile Creek: today, more water flows through the canal than through many of Ontario's natural rivers.

To this day, lines of trees offer evidence of the course of earlier canals. North of the Escarpment, the present waterway's high embankments, also bordered by tall trees, resemble long bluffs. Fourth Canal spoil, left near Lock 3, created a miniature mountain, now Pick Leeson Park.

Each of the canals cut off small streams, resulting in ponds, one of which now forms part of Mud Lake Wildlife Management Area [Fig. 2]. And water diverted from the canal to Ontario Hydro's plant on Twelve Mile Creek created lakes Gibson and Moodie on the Escarpment crest, the latter of which supplies water for the DeCew Generating Station [Fig. 3].

10.3 South of St. Catharines, ca. 1915: *What is now the DeCew Generating Station No. 1, constructed at the Escarpment, 1897-1899, created an artificial lake (Moodie) and fall of water. The plant still uses water diverted from the canal.*
Ontario Hydro

The shorelines of both Lake Ontario and Lake Erie were dramatically altered by the man-made harbours, first at Port Dalhousie and Port Colborne and later at Port Weller. While the mouth of Twelve Mile Creek at Port Dalhousie was wide enough to provide a good, safe harbour, ships entering the waterway still had to be protected from lake storms. The solution to this problem was to build breakwaters stretching out into Lake Ontario. Once into the shallow harbour, ships encountered shifting silt, a hazard overcome by construction of a towpath to define a channel which could be dredged [Figs. 4, 5]. The St. Lawrence Seaway Authority has already acquired land east of the present canal (between Thorold and Lake Ontario) in which "super-locks" may one day be constructed, each with a lift of over 80 feet (24 m).

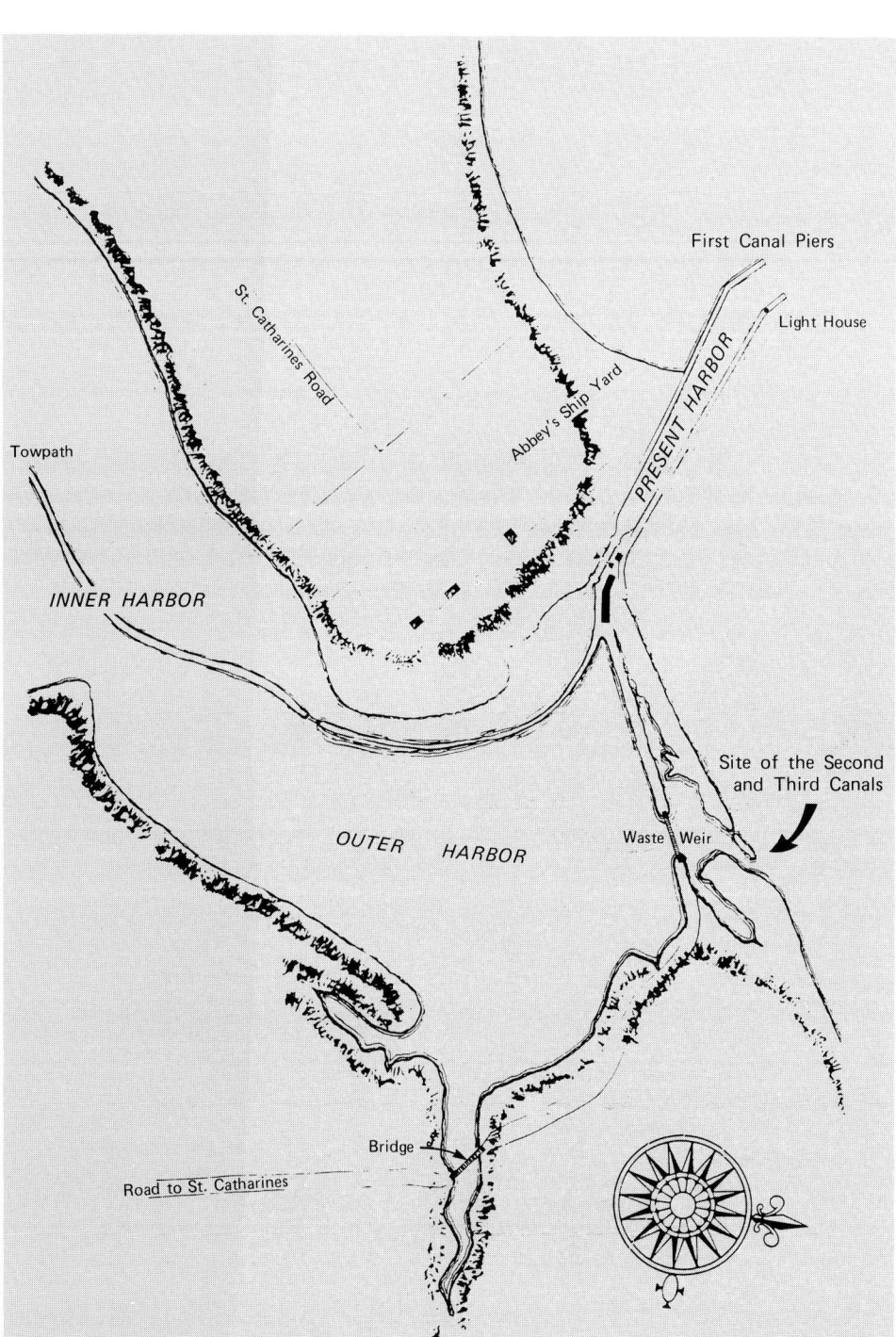

10.4 Port Dalhousie, ca. 1830: *Original map touched up to show entrances to the first three canals. Because the original piers were angled in a northwest direction (making it difficult for ships to get out of the harbour against the wind), the breakwaters of the Second and Third Canals projected in a more northerly direction.*

Map Library, Brock University, retouched by Loris Gasparotto

10.5 Port Dalhousie, ca. 1880: *The shed and cattle in the foreground are approximately on the site of the mouth and piers of the First Canal. The piers of the Second Canal run straight out, northward, into Lake Ontario. They in turn were replaced in the later 1880s by the piers which still protect the pleasure craft of the Port Dalhousie Yacht Club and remain notable features of the landscape.*
SCHM: N-3673 (*Picturesque Canada*, 1882)

10.6 Port Weller, 1934: *When the northern terminus of the canal was moved to the mouth of the Ten Mile Creek (Port Weller) in 1932, a new harbour was created by the breakwaters, themselves another impressive addition to the landscape. Excavated material from lock sites at the Escarpment was moved here by horsecarts and later by a special railway line.*
Canada. Dept. of Energy, Mines, and Resources

No creek flowed into Lake Erie to provide a natural harbour for a southern terminus to the canal [Fig. 7]. To make a choice, some directors of the Welland Canal Company "traversed the entire line" from Dunnville to Gravelly Bay in three spring days in 1831, inspected various possibilities, examined engineers' reports recommending Gravelly Bay, and sent two directors to examine and report further on this site. Gravelly Bay was chosen over the mouth of the Grand River as the shortest (12 miles/19 km), most direct and cheapest site, relative to Port Robinson. It was later named Port Colborne, where a slightly different solution to the problem of protection from lake storms was used, as breakwaters were built as independent units in Lake Erie [Fig. 8].

The effect of the canals on the urbanization of the Niagara Peninsula has already been shown (Chap. 6): new communities developed, old ones disappeared or declined, changing the look of the area in the process. Moreover, the symbiosis of canals and communities had to accommodate – and be accommodated by – land transportation. Roads and, later, railways had to cross the canal, necessitating bridges and/or tunnels [Fig. 9].

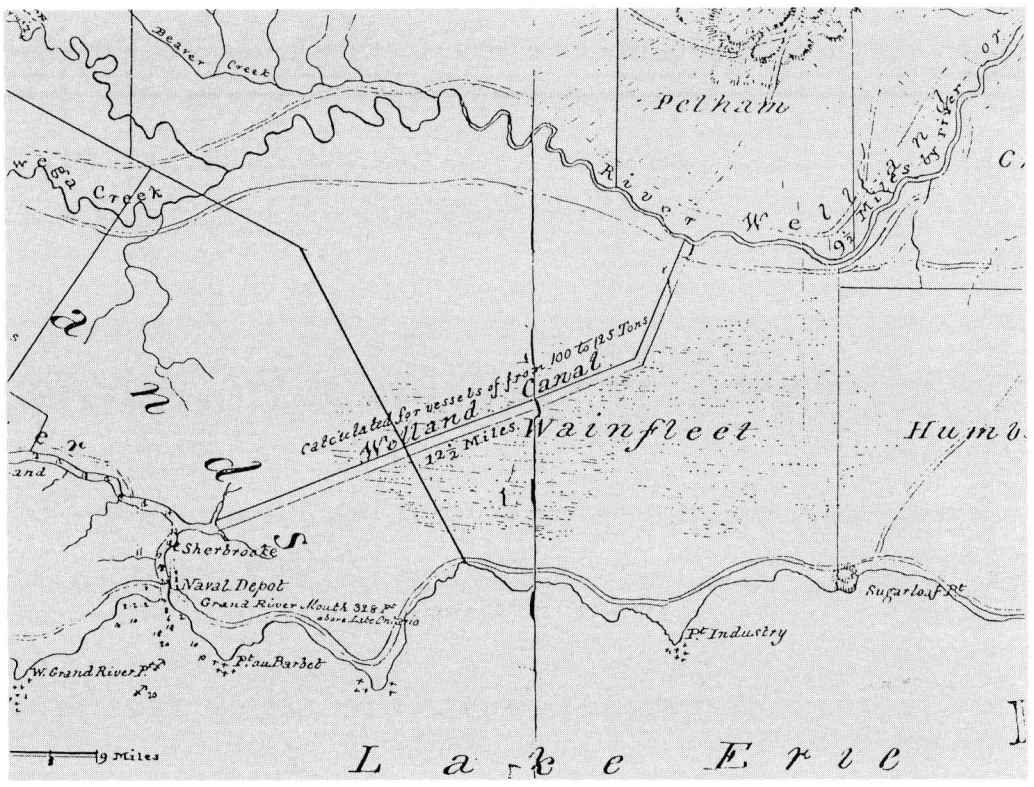

10.7 Lake Erie Shoreline, 1827: *A military map of the area from Humberstone to the Grand River indicates the difficulty in locating a southern terminus.*   Map Library, Brock University

10.8 Port Colborne, 1955 (opposite, top): *The Second and Third Canal locks are visible at the bridges; modern grain elevators are on the spit of land projecting out into the lake, left of the canal's mouth; the large property belonging to INCO is just off camera to right.*   Ontario. Ministry of Natural Resources

10.9 Welland, ca. 1975 (opposite, bottom): *This man-made waterscape illustrates two basic problems: how to resolve the conflicts between a) natural and artificial waterways, and b) land and water routes. In the centre of the picture, the Welland River is taken under the Fourth Canal through a syphon culvert, at approximately the site of the two earlier stone aqueducts (see Chap. 2, Figs. 7, 9, 10). At the upper right, another syphon culvert takes the river under the 1973 By-Pass. With construction of the By-Pass, all of the area conflict between land traffic and the canal was eliminated by the use of tunnels – in marked contrast to the Fourth Canal, which in Welland alone is crossed by several bridges.*   Canada. Dept. of Energy, Mines, and Resources

143

Ever since the First Canal cut its way across the peninsula, bridges have been a distinctive aspect of the landscape. But when goods travelled from east to west in small volume (and then usually by horse or oxen), and only the rich travelled for pleasure, crossing the waterway was not much of a problem [Fig. 10]. By the 1880s, with an increasing volume of road traffic and the coming of the railways, more crossings were required, and the conflict became ever more noticeable [Fig. 11]. By the end of the 19th century, increasing ship sizes necessitated the deepening and widening of the canals, and wooden bridges were no longer suitable. At the same time, improvements in iron and steel manufacture made steel bridges more feasible. By this time, too, the expansion of transport of goods and urban development were combining to increase the conflict between the needs of water and land traffic.

10.10 Welland, 1870: *A small, wooden, hand-operated drawbridge crossed the Second Canal, adequate for the low-volume local traffic on the unpaved road.*   John Burtniak Coll.

10.11 Port Robinson, ca. 1914: *A typical Third Canal-era swing bridge opens to let one of the last sailing vessels through, towed by a steam tug. In the late 1920s it would be replaced by a tall lift bridge [see Chap. 9, Fig. 11].*   John Burtniak Coll.

However, it was not only traffic that came into conflict in crossing the canal. The need to send hydro-electric transmission wires over the Second Canal resulted in construction of what were then the world's highest concrete structures [Fig. 12]. A more typical solution than St. Catharines' concrete poles were the now familiar steel skeleton towers, to be seen marching across the landscape [Fig. 13].

10.12 St. Catharines, 1902: *Concrete poles over 150 feet (46 m) high, built by the Concrete Pole Company for the Lincoln Electric Light and Power Co., stood by Lock 3, near the Glenridge Bridge, landmarks destroyed in 1971.* John Burtniak Coll.

10.13 Thorold, ca. 1932: *Steel skeleton towers (rear) near the lift bridge for Glendale Avenue carry electric power. At Lock 4 a double jack-knife bridge for the C. N. R. is up for the ships: three problems, three different solutions.* SCHM: N-7364

The lift bridges of the Fourth Canal are a distinctive feature of the Niagara landscape [see Fig. 21, and Chap. 7, Figs. 9, 13, 16, 24], but they also can be a frequent annoyance, as land traffic is disrupted by the passage of ships. The Garden City Skyway, allowing a free flow of land traffic over the waterway at St. Catharines, is a newer — and less disruptive — landmark [Figs. 14, 15].

10.14 Homer (Near St. Catharines), ca. 1950: *Congestion undreamed of by Merritt: backed-up cars and trucks begin to move again after a 20-minute wait, while Bridge 4 was up for the passage of a ship. Traffic on the east-west Queen Elizabeth Way (Canada's first four-lane divided highway, opened 1939) rapidly increased with the post-World War II boom, causing frequent bottlenecks.* SCHM: N-2339

10.15 The same scene, ca. 1975: *The solution to the problem was the Garden City Skyway (1963), carrying east-west traffic well above the masts of ships passing through the canal. Queues at Bridge 4 are much shorter now, affecting mainly local traffic and visitors to the Shaw Festival at Niagara-on-the-Lake. (Bridge 4 remains the only double-leaf rolling lift on the Fourth Canal.)* Alfred F. Sagon-King

If most water/ground conflicts were solved by taking ground transport *over* the canal, such has not always been the case, particularly in the Thorold area. While not as immediately obvious as the bridges, tunnels have been used since the 1880s, when the Grand Trunk Railway was routed through a magnificent tunnel constructed of hand-cut Queenston limestone blocks [Fig. 16]. More recently, three remarkable tunnels were constructed between 1965 and 1973 to carry road and rail lines under the waterway. Those at Thorold and at Main St. in Welland are just for highways [Fig. 17]; the Townline Tunnel in Welland carries railways as well.

10.16 Thorold, ca. 1885: *The 650-foot (198 m) tunnel, over 18 feet (5 m) high, is separated from the water of Lock 18 by less than three feet (1 m) of earth. Water still flows over the disused tunnel (see Chap. 2, Fig. 17).*
PAC: C-20630

10.17 Thorold, ca. 1970: *In the mid-1960s twin tubes replaced two bridges to allow Highway 58 to pass under the canal. This tunnel was constructed over three winters, when the canal was de-watered (see also Fig. 9).*   H.R. Oakman

Bridges, towers, tunnels: all have contributed to the special look of the Niagara landscape, and all were unlikely developments without the Welland Canals. Buildings associated with the canals have also contributed to that special look: lockmasters' houses [see Chap. 6, Fig.14], tow-horse barns, labourers' amenities [see Chap. 6, Fig.13], factories, mills [Fig. 18], warehouses, businesses, terminus facilities – not to mention the grand residences of canal-prosperous entrepreneurs, many of whom built spacious houses, often on the hillside where they could overlook the busy waterway [Fig. 19].

10.18 Merritton, ca. 1910: *The many mills and factories (such as that of the Independent Rubber Company, built 1882) have been, and still are, a distinctive aspect of the landscape. Only the annex, with its tall smokestack, survives – still a landmark on Glendale Avenue.*   SCHM: N-1077

10.19 St. Catharines, ca. 1865: *Some canal-side mansions survive. This magnificent home, for example, built by Thomas Rodman Merritt between 1853 and 1863, and now (as "Rodman Hall") serving as an art gallery for the city of St. Catharines. No longer does the canal pass by, but the building is a lasting reminder of the area's canal legacy.*   SCHM: N-4962

The present canal, like its forerunners, provides jobs, attracts business and tourist dollars, and is fascinating simply by itself. But it also slices through communities, creates noise, air and water pollution, and obstructs land traffic (see Chap. 9 and above). Niagara residents today are perhaps more aware than ever of the importance of the Welland Canal to their lives, whether for good or ill. On the whole, citizen response has been largely positive. And in the 20th century there has been increasing realization of the historical importance of the canals [Fig. 20].

From 1929, the centenary of the opening of the First Canal, through the Canadian Centennial celebrations in 1967, to the 150th anniversary of the opening of the waterway in 1979, local residents have become ever more aware of the significance of the canals to their communities, the blessings and the difficulties [Fig. 21].

The nature of the problems changes over time, but the man-made waterway itself is here to stay. As we approach the 21st century, we must be prepared for the ongoing presence of the Welland Canal — in whatever form it may evolve. Its effects are now the concern of geographers and geologists, experts in traffic control, land use and pollution, urban planners and sociologists, to say nothing of shipbuilders and shipping companies the world over. For better or worse, the Welland Canal will undoubtedly continue in its role as creator of both prosperity and problems, and as transformer of the Niagara Peninsula.

10.20 Port Dalhousie, 1971: *Even more directly related to the canal are the lighthouses on the east pier (the outer one built in 1879; the inner in 1898). Functional and essential for the safety of ships, they also continue to give the old northern terminus its own sense of place, as part of a unique heritage. At the same time they are providing picturesque testimony to the role the Welland Canal has played in transforming a landscape.*
Alfred F. Sagon-King

10.21 Near Dain City, 1969: *The pilot of the TADOUSSAC had to direct his vessel very carefully through an opening at Bridge 18 which, while it sufficed in the 1930s, is a hazard for the larger ships of the later 20th century. Although the projecting support structures can cause difficulty, the bridge itself is a permanent feature of the Niagara Peninsula landscape.* Alfred F. Sagon-King

Aft.1 St. Catharines, 1929: *On St. Paul Street, not far from his home, William Hamilton Merritt's statue (commissioned by his descendants) overlooks the route of the First and Second Canals. He appears to be gazing south, past Thorold and Allanburg, Port Robinson and Welland, to Port Colborne. These canal communities and their industries, their people and their way of life, are also monuments to Merritt's vision, determination and dedication to opening up the heartland of North America to communication with the wider world.*
SCHM: N-4784

AFTERWORD: THE FUTURE OF THE PAST

The growing awareness of the importance of the Welland Canal to the Niagara Peninsula communities has led to two separate, but related, activities over the years. On the one hand, various groups have set up monuments and plaques to commemorate people and events of significance to Niagara's development. Among the earliest were the cairn at Allanburg and the Merritt statue in St. Catharines [see Fig. 1]. More recently, provincial and local authorities have erected markers at Port Dalhousie, Welland, Port Colborne, and in other canal communities, both on the present waterway and along the remnants of the Second Canal.

On the other hand, some groups have established ongoing projects to restore, preserve and develop historic features of the waterway. For example, in 1978 the St. Catharines Historical Museum, with federal government support, and aid and assistance from several local groups, sponsored the development of Mountain Locks Park, where the First and Second Canals "climbed the mountain" at Merritton. In 1977 the most ambitious project to date was launched: the Welland Canals Preservation Association, who formulated the concept of a linear park along the old canal lands, from Port Dalhousie to Port Colborne. Their plan includes restoring locks [Fig. 2] and other canal-related structures [Fig. 8], and linking them by a walking and hiking trail, with picnic sites and historical markers at appropriate locations. Generously assisted by local and provincial government grants, by Niagara businesses, and by the volunteer labour of scores of citizens, the W.C.P.A. completed the "Merritt Trail" from Port Dalhousie to Port Colborne in 1986 [Fig. 3].

Aft.2 St. Catharines, September 1985: *Lock 17 of the Second Canal, restored by the Welland Canals Preservation Association as part of Mountain Locks Park. Members of the Canadian Canal Society and the St. Catharines Historical Museum discuss restoration along the Welland Canal with a touring group from the Inland Waterways Association of Great Britain.* R.M. Styran

Similar work is proceeding in most canal communities. For instance, in Dunnville and Wainfleet, the Rehabilitate the Old Feeder Canal Association, founded in 1979, is restoring the almost forgotten channel from the Grand River to the Welland River. Through their efforts, scenes such as that in Chapter 8, Figure 26, may once again become common.

Aft.3 St. Catharines, 1985: *The Merritt Trail runs along the series of locks, providing facilities for hiking, jogging and picnicking in summer, and cross-country skiing in winter.*   R.R. Taylor

Aft.4 Port Dalhousie, 1979 (left): *A replica of the ANNIE AND JANE of York (one of the two schooners which inaugurated the canal in 1829) arrives to help Niagara residents celebrate the sesquicentennial of the opening of the first Welland Canal. Increasingly, Niagara's canal network and its related festivities attract visitors from all over Canada, the United States and overseas [see Fig. 2].*
Anne Taylor

Also in 1979, the group now known as the Welland Canals Foundation organized the 150th anniversary celebrations of the opening of Merritt's "ditch", and promoted the occasion with Niagara-wide celebrations. Among many festive events, a replica of the schooner ANNIE AND JANE sailed into Port Dalhousie [Fig. 4]. "Canal Days" are now held annually on the waterway under their auspices. Publicity, publications, conferences and educational programmes have been sponsored, including a St. Catharines actor playing William Hamilton Merritt in canal communities and throughout Ontario, Canada and parts of the United States [see Chap. 1, Fig. 16]. One episode of the TV Ontario series "Behind the Shield" featured "Mr. Merritt" and the Welland Canal.

More recently (1986), representatives of local canal heritage groups formed the Welland Canals Society to develop the Canal corridor, including a continuous scenic drive, as part of a Welland Canals Parkway. Both the Welland Canals Preservation Association and the Welland Canals Society have involved not only various levels of government and local heritage groups, but also local business organizations, service groups, Chambers of Commerce and the Regional Tourist Council in their efforts. Such co-operative planning may well prove to be a model for other areas.

As well, local museums, such as the Port Colborne Historical and Marine Museum (opened 1975), have become assiduous in preserving canal artifacts and lore [Fig. 5]. Consciousness of the waterway's importance motivated the Port Dalhousie Quorum's Heritage Committee to found Heritage St. Catharines, a "grass-roots" citizens' group concerned to restore and protect valuable older structures in this central canal city [Fig. 6].

Aft.5 Port Colborne, 1982: *The Port Colborne Historical and Marine Museum occupies a former grocery store, built in 1869. The museum has also preserved and restored several other old structures, as well as pictures and artifacts, and is a focal point for the annual summer "Canal Days" celebrations.*   PCHMM

Aft.6 Port Dalhousie, 1987: *Originally the office of the Muir Brothers Dry Dock, and renovated by local residents, Dalhousie House now functions as a community centre. It was the headquarters of the Welland Canals Preservation Association from 1978 to 1987.*   R.R. Taylor

It was perhaps fitting that Port Dalhousie, the northern terminus of the first three canals (i.e., from 1829 to 1932), was the site of the founding of the Canadian Canal Society in 1982. Dedicated to the preservation and use of Canada's historic canals, the Society has a growing membership and a fine future. In the heart of the peninsula, the federal government and the Welland Canal Parkway Board developed the abandoned Fourth Canal as a recreational park. As well, the Welland Heritage Council has been active, working to preserve and restore the area's unique canal inheritance.

The Welland Canal's value to the economy (not merely local and regional, but also national — even international) is enormous and long recognized. But only recently have the series of man-made waterways which traverse the peninsula been appreciated as a *potentially valuable resource in themselves*, for both education and recreation. Our transformed landscape is now seen as a priceless heritage, and one which, as befits its long tradition, has tremendous potential as a continuing source of prosperity, drawing tourists and canal buffs from near and far. As the whole St. Lawrence Seaway faces increasing competition from both the Mississippi waterway and the trucking and railway industries, it may well be that the commercial importance of the Welland Canal will be overshadowed by its role as an educational and recreational resource [Figs. 7, 8].

THE OLD KNIFE WORKS

Aft.7 St. Catharines, 1987: *Part of the Whitman Barnes Manufacturing Company (1870), between Locks 5 and 6 of the Second Canal, has been converted for use as the headquarters of the Welland Canals Society, as well as for the Welland Canals Preservation Association, which will continue its pioneering efforts to help preserve Niagara's canal heritage.*   Welland Canals Society

Aft.8 Port Dalhousie, 1982 (below): *As part of their overall plans, the W.C.P.A. created Lock One Park (opened 1981) on the site of the Second Canal lock. A retired welder contributed a decorative iron fence to commemorate the men and animals whose labours were essential to the construction of the first three canals, of which Port Dalhousie was the northern terminus.*   R.R. Taylor

FIRST WELLAND CANAL
STARTED 1824 —— COMPLETED 1829

TYPICAL VESSEL
LENGTH 100 FT. - CARGO CAPACITY 185 TONS

TYPICAL LOCK

LENGTH BETWEEN GATES .... 110 FT.
WIDTH OF LOCK .... 22 FT.
DEPTH OF WATER OVER SILLS ...... 8 FT.
SINGLE LIFTS .... 6 FT. TO 11 FT.
NUMBER OF LOCKS 39

SECOND WELLAND CANAL
STARTED 1842 —— COMPLETED 1845

TYPICAL VESSEL
LENGTH 140 FT. - CARGO CAPACITY 750 TONS

TYPICAL LOCK

LENGTH BETWEEN GATES .... 150 FT.
WIDTH OF LOCK .... 26 FT. 6 IN.
DEPTH OF WATER OVER SILLS ...... 9 FT.
SINGLE LIFTS ..... 9 FT. 6 IN. TO 14 FT. 3 IN.
NUMBER OF LOCKS 27

THIRD WELLAND CANAL
STARTED 1875 —— COMPLETED 1887

TYPICAL VESSEL
LENGTH 255 FT - CARGO CAPACITY 2700 TONS

TYPICAL LOCK

LENGTH BETWEEN GATES .... 270 FT.
WIDTH OF LOCK .... 45 FT.
DEPTH OF WATER OVER SILLS ..... 14 FT.
SINGLE LIFTS .... 12 FT. TO 16 FT.
NUMBER OF LOCKS 26

WELLAND SHIP CANAL
STARTED 1913 —— COMPLETED 1932-33

LENGTH BETWEEN INNER GATES ___ 859 FT.
WIDTH OF LOCK _____ 80 FT.
DEPTH OF WATER OVER SILLS ____ 30 FT. (REACHES 25 FT)

SINGLE LIFTS _____ 46 FT. 6 IN.
NUMBER OF LOCKS _ INCLUDING 3 TWIN _____ 8
TOTAL LOCKAGE _____ 325 FT. 6 IN.

THE GUARD LOCK AT HUMBERSTONE IS 1380 FT. LONG BETWEEN INNER GATES

TYPICAL LOCK

TYPICAL VESSEL
MAXIMUM LENGTH 820 FT. & CARGO CAPACITY 25000 TONS AT 24 FT. DRAFT.

The Welland Canals, 1932: *This diagram celebrated what must have seemed the final answer to the changing technology of shipbuilding. Yet within 30 years a section of the Fourth Canal had to be rebuilt and expanded as part of the continuing epic of construction and reconstruction. Today, the Welland is the "bottleneck" of the St. Lawrence Seaway.* Cowan, Frontispiece

APPENDIX

We have frequently been asked about statistical details regarding the size and capacity of the locks of the successive Welland Canals. The following figures are based on those provided by Percy J. Cowan, in the frontispiece to *The Welland Ship Canal between Lake Erie and Lake Ontario, 1913-1932* (Reprint of Articles Appearing in "Engineering." London: Office of "Engineering," 1935), and by Charles H. Atkinson, "Aspects of Engineering on the Welland Canals," in *The Welland Canals. Proceedings of the First Annual Niagara Peninsula History Conference*. St. Catharines: Brock University, 1979, pp. 35-64.

FIRST WELLAND CANAL

Typical Vessels	—length:	100 feet (30.5 m)
	—tonnage:	185 tons*
Locks (40, wood)	—length:	110 feet (33.5 m) between gates
	—width:	22 feet (6.7 m)
Single Lifts	—6-11 feet (1.8-3.4 m)	

SECOND WELLAND CANAL

Typical Vessels	—length:	140 feet (42.7 m)
	—tonnage:	750 tons*
Locks (27, cut stone)	—length:	150 feet (45.7 m)
	—width:	26.5 feet (8.1 m)
Single Lifts	—9.5-14.25 feet (2.9-4.3 m)	

THIRD WELLAND CANAL

Typical Vessels	—length:	255 feet (77.7 m)
	—tonnage:	3,000 tons*
Locks (26, cut stone)	—length:	270 feet (82.3 m)
	—width:	45 feet (13.8 m)
Single Lifts	—12-16 feet (3.6-4.9 m)	

WELLAND SHIP CANAL (FOURTH CANAL)

Typical Vessel	—length:	730 feet (222.5 m)**
	—tonnage:	25,000 tons*
Locks (7, concrete)	—length:	859 feet (261.8 m) betweeen inner gates
(an additional guard lock at Port Colborne is 1380 feet/350 m in length)		
	—width:	80 feet (24.3 m)
Single Lifts	—47.9 feet (14.6 m)	

* Tonnage of ships is not given in metric figures because vessels are not yet required to be registered in metric.

** Cowan erroneously gives the typical length of vessels as 820 feet.

ABBREVIATIONS

AO	Archives of Ontario
Canada	Canada. Department of Railways and Canals. *Opening of the Welland Ship Canal, August 6, 1932*. Ottawa: King's Printer, 1932.
Centennial	*St. Catharines Centennial History*. St. Catharines: Advance Printing, 1967.
Cowan	P.J. Cowan. *The Welland Ship Canal between Lake Ontario and Lake Erie 1913-1932*. London: Offices of "Engineering," 1935.
Cuthbertson	George Cuthbertson. *Freshwater. A History and Narrative of the Great Lakes*. Toronto: Macmillan, 1931.
DeVolpi	Charles P. deVolpi. *The Niagara Peninsula: A Pictorial Record*. Don Mills: Longmans, 1966.
Harper's	Frederic G. Mather, "Water Routes from the Great North West," *Harper's New Monthly Magazine*, lxiii (1881), 415-435.
JNJ	John N. Jackson. *St. Catharines, Ontario: Its Early Years*. Belleville: Mika, 1976.
Keefer	Thomas C. Keefer. *The Old Welland Canal and the Man Who Built It*. St. Catharines: The Print Shop, 1920.
PAC	Public Archives of Canada (now, National Archives of Canada)
Page's *Atlas*	H.R. Page. *Illustrated Historical Atlas of the Counties of Lincoln and Welland*, 1876.
PCHMM	Port Colborne Historical and Marine Museum
SCHM	St. Catharines Historical Museum
Traveller	*The Northern Traveller: Containing the Routes of Niagara, Quebec, and the Springs with the Tour of New England and the Route to the Coal Mines of Pennsylvania*. New York: A.T. Goodrich, 1926, pp. 77, 99.
Tremaine	Tremaine's *Map of the Counties of Lincoln and Welland, Canada West*. Toronto: 1862.
Tuer	J.A. Tuer. *An Historical Narrative of Some Important Events....* Toronto: United Church Publishing House, 1931.
Ware	Michael E. Ware. *England's Lost Waterways(1)*. Moorland, 1979.
Wellandward	Welland Board of Trade. *Turn Wellandward*. Welland *Telegraph*, 1921.

NOTES

Preface:

1. Photographers whose work we have used include George Adrian Cuthbertson (fl. ca. 1885), John Williams (fl. 1912-19), John Boyd (fl. 1880-1930), J.W. Jarrett (fl. 1919-20), J.A. McDonald (fl. 1921-29), and James Joy (fl. 1929-32).

Introduction:

2. J.P. Merritt, *Biography of the Hon. W.H. Merritt, M.P....* . St. Catharines: Leavenworth, 1875, p. 123. (Henceforth cited as *Biography*.)

3. Upper Canada Assembly, *Journals*, 1818. Cited in *Tenth Report of the Bureau of Archives of the Province of Ontario for 1913*. Toronto: King's Printer, 1914. Vol. 4, p. 218.

4. *Ibid.*

5. Upper Canada Assembly, *Journals*, 1836-37. Appendix II, 90, p. 219. Third Report from the Select Committee Appointed to Examine and Enquire into the Management of the Welland Canal, quoting a press circular of 1st September 1824.

6. Quoted in Anthony Burton, *The Canal Builders*. Newton Abbott: David and Charles, 1981, pp. 3-4.

7. *Despatches, Correspondence, and Memoranda of Field Marshall Arthur Duke of Wellington, K.G.*, edited by his son, the Duke of Wellington, K.G. 8 vols. London: John Murray, 1867-73. Vol. 1, p. 39.

8. *The Dispatches of Field Marshal the Duke of Wellington...1799 to 1815.* Compiled by Lieut. Colonel [John] Gurwood. 13 vols. London: John Murray, 1837-39. Vol. 11, p. 525.

Chapter 1:

9. *Biography*, p. 96.

10. *Ibid.*, p. 57.

11. *Ibid.*, p. 61.

12. *Ibid.*, p. 116.

13. *Ibid.*, p. 119.

14. *Ibid.*, p. 125.

15. William Kingsford, *The Canadian Canals: Their History and Cost....* Toronto: Rollo and Adam, 1865, p. 61.

16. *Biography*, p. 57.

17. At the sod-turning ceremony, 30 November 1824. Quoted in *Biography*, p. 66.

18. Letter to his father-in-law, Jedediah Prendergast, 13 January. Quoted in H.G.J. Aitken, *The Welland Canal Company: A Study in Canadian Enterprise.* Cambridge, Mass.: Harvard University Press, 1954, p. 54.

19. Aitken, *op. cit.*, p. 30.

20. *Biography*, p. 67.

Chapter 3:

21. Upper Canada. House of Assembly. *Journal of Proceedings. Appendix: First Report of the Select Committee of the Upper Canada Legislature Appointed to Report upon the Several Petitions to the President of the Welland Canal Company....* 15 December 1825, p. 11.

22. Elting E. Morison, *From Know-How to Nowhere: The Development of American Technology.* New York: New American Library, 1974, p. 35.

23. E.A. Cruikshank, "The Inception of the Welland Canal," *Ontario Historical Society Papers and Records,* XXII (1925), p. 79. Cruikshank printed excerpts from the Coventry Papers as "The Narrative of William Hamilton Merritt," including letters and Welland Canal Company notices.

24. "Junius," "A Walk around the Town: W continued," in *St. Catharines, A to Z.* [St. Catharines]: St. Catharines and Lincoln Historical Society, 1967, n.p.

25. Cruikshank, *op. cit.,* p. 35.

26. William H. Smith, *Smith's Canadian Gazetteer....* Toronto: H. & W. Rowsell, 1846, p. 207.

27. Canal Commission. Letter to the Honorable the Secretary of State from the Canal Commissioners respecting the Improvement of the Inland Navigation of the Dominion of Canada. Ottawa: 24th February, 1871, p. 59.

28. George A. Rawlyk, "Thomas Coltrin Keefer and the St. Lawrence-Great Lakes Commercial System," in *Inland Seas,* Vol. 19, No. 3 (1963), p. 191.

Chapter 4:

29. "Junius," "A Walk around Town: O," in *St. Catharines, A to Z.* [St. Catharines]: St. Catharines and Lincoln Historical Society, 1967, n.p.

30. J.J. Talman, "The Impact of the Welland Canals on the Community," in *The Welland Canals. Proceedings of the First Annual Niagara Peninsula History Conference.* St. Catharines: Brock University, 1979, p. 84.

31. John N. Jackson, *St. Catharines, Ontario: Its Early Years.* Belleville: Mika, 1976, pp. 222-23.

Chapter 6:

32. William Richard Harris, *The Catholic Church in the Niagara Peninsula, 1626-1895.* Toronto: Briggs, 1895, p. 260.

33. J.Lawrence Runnalls, *The Irish on the Welland Canal.* St. Catharines: St. Catharines Public Library, 1973, p. 6.

34. *Ibid,* pp. 13-15.

Chapter 7:

35. *Biography,* p. 77.

36. *Ibid.,* p. 143.

Chapter 8:

37. *Ibid.,* in a letter to her parents, 24 March 1829.

38. An Emigrant Farmer [Joseph Abbot], *The Emigrant to North America....* Edinburgh: Blackwood, 1844, p. 74. Quoted in Jackson, *op. cit.,* p. 239.

39. *St. Catharines Journal,* 21 July 1853. Quoted in Jackson, *ibid.,* p. 317.

Chapter 9:

40. Recollections of a worker, 29 years old at the time of the 1928 disaster, in "Niagara Summertime Tours," a typescript of taped interviews, 1977 (tape 1, p.1).

41. *Biography,* p. 81.

42. *The Globe and Mail* (Toronto), "Report on Business," 6 November 1985, p. B13.

43. St. Catharines *Standard,* 8 August 1932, p. 1.

SELECT BIBLIOGRAPHY

Aitken, H.G.J. *The Welland Canal Company. A Study in Canadian Enterprise.* Cambridge, Mass.: Harvard University Press, 1954.

Bleasdale, Ruth Elisabeth. *Irish Labourers on the Cornwall, Welland and Williamsburg Canals in the 1840s.* University of Western Ontario, 1975 (M.A. thesis).

Burtniak, John, and Wesley B. Turner (eds.). *The Welland Canals. Proceedings of the First Annual Niagara Peninsula History Conference.* St. Catharines: Brock University, 1979.

Canada. Department of Railways and Canals. *The Opening of the Welland Ship Canal, August sixth, nineteen thirty-two.* Ottawa: King's Printer, 1932.

Cowan, P.J. *The Welland Ship Canal Between Lake Ontario and Lake Erie, 1913-1932.* London: Offices of "Engineering," 1935.

Cruikshank, E.A. "The Inception of the Welland Canal," *Ontario Historical Society Papers and Records,* XXII (1925).

Duquemin, Colin K. *The Historic Welland Canals,* parts 1 and 2. Welland: Niagara South Board of Education, 1979.

Duquemin, Colin K., and Daniel J. Glenney. *A Guide to the Grand River Canal.* St. Catharines: St. Catharines Historical Museum, 1980. (Publication No. 1)

Gilham, E.B. ("Skip"). *Ships Along the Seaway.* 2 vols. Fonthill, Ontario: Stonehouse, 1971, 1975.

Greenwald, Michelle et al. *The Welland Canals. Historical Resource Analysis and Preservation Alternatives.* Ontario. Ministry of Culture and Recreation. Historical Planning and Research. Heritage Branch Conservation Division, 1977.

Heisler, John P. *Canals of Canada.* Ottawa: Canada. Department of Indian Affairs and Northern Development, 1973. (Canadian Historic Sites: Occasional Papers in Archaeology and History, No. 8)

Jackson, John N. *St. Catharines, Ontario. Its Early Years.* Belleville: Mika, 1976.

Jackson, John N. *Welland and the Welland Canal: The Welland Canal By-Pass.* Belleville: Mika, 1975.

Jackson, John N., and Fred A. Addis. *The Welland Canals. A Comprehensive Guide.* St. Catharines: Lincoln Graphics (for the Welland Canals Foundation), 1982.

Keefer, Thomas C. *The Old Welland Canal and the Man Who Made It.* St. Catharines: The Print Shop, 1920.

Kingsford, William. *The Canadian Canals. Their History and Cost.* Toronto: Rollo and Adam, 1865.

Leggett, Robert F. *Canals of Canada.* Vancouver: Douglas, David & Charles, 1976.

Meaney, Carl Frank Patrick. *The Welland Canal and Canadian Development.* Hamilton: McMaster University, 1980 (M.A. thesis).

Merritt, Jedediah P. *Biography of the Hon. W.H. Merritt, M.P.* St. Catharines: Leavenworth, 1875.

Michener, David M. *The Canals at Welland.* Welland: Rotary Club of Welland, 1973.

Page, H.R. *Illustrated Historical Atlas of the Counties of Lincoln and Welland, Ont.* Toronto: Craig, Steam Litho, 1876 (reprinted, Port Elgin: Cumming, 1971).

Runnalls, J. Lawrence. *The Irish on the Welland Canals.* St. Catharines: St. Catharines Public Library, 1974.

St. Catharines Historical Museum. *A Canadian Enterprise. The Welland Canals. The "Merritt Day" Lectures, 1978-82.* St. Catharines: St. Catharines Historical Museum, 1984. (Publication No. 4)

Sayles, Fern A. *Welland Workers Make History.* Welland, 1963.

Styran, Roberta M., and Robert R. Taylor. "The Welland Canal. Creator of a Landscape," *Ontario History,* LXXII, no. 4 (December 1980), 210-229.

Taylor, Robert Stanley. *The Historical Development of the Four Welland Canals, 1824-1933.* London: University of Western Ontario, 1950 (M.A. thesis).

"Water Routes from the Great North West," *Harper's New Monthly Magazine,* LXIII (August 1880), 415-435.

INDEX

Accidents, **126**, 127, 130, **131**, **132**, 133, **135**, 136
Adams, George, 20, **21**
Allan, Hon. William, 24, 106
Allanburg, **29**, 34, 36, 64, **106**, 121, 124, **131**, 136
Aqueduct (place), 34, 104; Aqueducts (canals), **xiv**, **xv**, 34, **35**, 36, 49, 113, 124, 142

Baldwin, Hon. Stanley, **54**
Bessborough, Earl of, Gov.-Gen., **54**
Boulton, D'Arcy, 24; Boulton, Henry John, 24
Bridges, 12, 35, 40, **41**, 70, 77, 79, 104, 109, **110**, 111, 113, 114, **119**, 130, 131, **135**, 142, **144**, **145**, **146**, 147, 148, **151**
Bridgewater, 3rd Duke of (Francis Egerton), **xv**

C.K.T.B., **99**
Canadian Canal Society, 153, 156
Canadian Furnace Co., 65
"Canal Days", 124, 154; "Canal Rats", (ca. 1920) **125**
Canals: Basingstoke (Eng.), 47; Bras d'Or, xiv; Burlington Bay, xiii; Canal du Midi, **xv-xvi**; Champlain, xvi; Chignecto, xvi; Göta, xiv; Languedoc, xvi; Rideau, ix, xvi; Santee (South Carolina), xvi; Shropshire Union (Eng.), **44**; Shubenacadie, xiv; *see also* Erie, Feeder, Welland
Carter's Store, **110**
Cavalry, W.W.I, **137**
Chippawa, **107**
Chisholm, William, 20, **21**
Civil War (U.S.), 136
Coalport (Eng.), **31**
Colborne, Sir John, Lt. Gov., 24, **25**
Concrete Pole Co., 145
Consolidated Rubber Factory, 100
Construction methods and materials, 43, 44, 47, 48, **49**, **50**, **53**, 85, 88, **68**, **91**, **95**, 127
Contractors: Beach, General, 44; Brown, John, **48**; Hovey, Alfred, 44; Phelps, Oliver, 44, **45**
Costs, 127, 128, 133, 134
Court House (Welland), **34**, (1860) 105
Cranberry Marsh, 34
Cronmiller and White, brewery, **122**

Customs and excise, (ca. 1878) **93**

Dain City, **151**
Dalhousie, 9th Earl of (George Ramsay), 23; Dalhousie House, **156**
Davenport Flour Mill, **57**
DeCew, John, 20; DeCew Falls, **21**, 31; DeCew Generating Station, **139**
Deep Cut, **36**, **37**, 44, 84, 113
Defence, **136**, **137**
Dept. Railways and Canals (Canada), 92
Dick's Creek, 139
Disease, 40, 85, 87, 127
Dobbie's Iron and Brass, 58, (ca. 1876) **59**
Dolphin Paint Works, **56**
Duffin's Inn, 87
Dunn, Hon. John Henry, 24, 105, 108; Dunnville, **34**, 73, 104, **108**, 125, 133, **134**, 142
Dwyer, James, 127
Dyer, C.J., 112

Economic potential, 26, 27
Electric Power: Hydro-electric Power, 67, 139, **145**
Emigration and immigration, 63, 84, 86, 88, 93
Engineers (British): Brindley, James, **xv**; Rennie, John, xiii; Telford, Thomas, xiii-**xiv**, 22, 25; Welland Canal: Baird, N.H., 42, 43; Grant, Alexander J., **54**, **55**, 127; Hall, Francis, **x**, xiii-xiv, 22; Keefer, Thomas Coltrin, 21, 50, **51**; Killaly, H.H., 42, 43; Roberts, Nathan, S., 22; Weller, John Laing, 54
Erie Canal, xiii, xvi, 22, **23**, **24**, 27, 43, 57, 86; Erie Park, 122

Family Compact, 24-25
Feeder Canal, **34**, 35, 37, 40, **104**, **125**, 133, 134, 154
Fenians, 136, **137**
Financing, 40, 47
Flight Locks (Thorold), ii, **28**, **32**, **33**, **41**, **42**, 53, 81, 103. *See also* Locks
Fraser Paper Mills, 59, 64, **103**

General Motors of Canada, 60
Garden City Skyway, **113**, **114**, 146, 147. *See also* Bridges
Grain elevator(s), 38, **62**, 66, 70, 73, 76, 79, 82, 109, 111, **117**, **142**
Grand River, 24, 34, 35, 108, **134**, 142, 154
Gravelly Bay, 123, 124, 142

Hay Incline (Eng.), **31**
Heritage St. Catharines, 155

Highway 406, 97
Hog Island, **107**
Homer, **113**, **114**, 130, 146, 147
Humberstone, 73, 109, **110**, **142**. *See also* Port Colborne
Hunt, Cairns and Co. Wheelworks, **56**
Hutchinson's Mill, **56**

Ice fishing, **121**; Ice jams, **133**; Ice merchants, **66**
Independent Rubber Co., **149**
Industry and Trade, 56, **57**, 58, 60, 63, 64, 65, 66, 67, 71, **96**, 99, 134
International Nickel Co. (INCO), 68, 142, **143**
Irish (on the Welland Canal), 86-87, 101; Italians (on the Welland Canal), 88

Keefer, George, xiii, 20, **21**, 29, 65, **103**; Keefer, Jacob, 59, 103; Keefer, John, 104

Labouring and labouring classes, 43, 48, 71, 84, 85, 90, 92, 94, **96**, 137
Lake Erie, 34, 35, 37, 109, **142**
Lake Moodie, **139**
Lakeside Park, **117**, **118**, 119
Lampreys, 136
Landscape features, 139; *see also* Niagara Escarpment
Lighthouses, **141**, **150**
Limestone, 44, 47, 48, 49, 52, 84, 148
Lincoln and Welland sawmill, **43**
Lincoln Electric Light and Power Co., 145
Lock One Park, **157**; Lock Seven Motel, 115
Lockport, N.Y., 27
Locks, **x**, xiii, **xv**, xvi, 27, 31, 44, 47, 50, 57, 95, 135, 140, 153; First Canal, **xi**, **xii**, 42, 43, 46, 86, **158**, **159**; Second Canal, **ix**, 30, 43, 47, 58, 59, 61, 65, 70, 71, 72, 93, 109, 111, 127, 134, 142, 153, 156, 157, 158, 159; Third Canal, 32, 38, 64, 66, 67, 77, 84, 95, 100, 109, 111, 112, 114, 116, 121, 124, 127, 129, 131, 142, 145, 148, 158, 159; Fourth Canal, ii, **28**, **33**, **41**, **52**, **53**, **54**, **55**, 74, 76, 78, 81, 88, 89, 90, 91, 94, 95, 103, 114, 115, 124, 126, **129**, 130, 132, 138, 139, 145, 158, 159
Locktenders, 92, 93, 95, 96, 124

McCalls'a Park, **129**
Mack, Dr. Theophilus, 98
Mackenzie, David, **29**
McKinnon, Lachlan E., **60**; McKinnon Dash and Hardware Co., **60**
Main St. (Welland), **105**
Maitland, Sir Peregrine, xiii, 24, 113

Maple Leaf Milling Co., 66; Maple Leaf Rubber Co., 100
Maplehurst (Thorold), 103
Maps and Diagrams: 18, 20, 21, 24, 29, 39, 42, 56, 105, 140, 142, 150, 158
Marshville, 113
Martindale Pond, 70, 118, 119
Merritt, J.P., 128; Merritt, Thomas, 21; Merritt, Thomas Rodman, 43, 149
Merritt, William Hamilton, xii, xiii, xiv, xv, xvi, 19, 20, 21, 22, 23, 27-28, 29, 43, 55, 60, 72, 98, 99, 152
Merritt, Mrs. William Hamilton, 109, 113
Merritt Trail, 124, 154
Merritton, 30, 42, 45, 46, 61, 64, 87, 92, 101, 120, 133, 134, 149, 153, 156
Merrittsville, 104
Mills, 42, 56, 57, 58, 59, 60, 63, 64, 65, 97, 133; *see also* individual names
Misener Transportation, 83
Monuments and Plaques, 106, 108, 126, 137, 152
Mountain Locks Park, 30, 134, 153
Mud Lake Wildlife Management Area, 124, 138, 139
Muir Bros. Dry Dock, 70, 72, 75, 100, 156
Murphy, Ed ("Murphy's"), 100

Neelon, Capt. Sylvester, 69, 96
Neptune's Staircase, 30, 42, 134
Newspapers/Journals: *Canadian Illustrated News*, ix; *Farmers' Journal and Welland Canal Intelligencer*, 26, 57; *Globe* (Toronto), 61; *Great Western Railway Gazetteer*, 62; *Picturesque Canada*, xiii; *St. Catharines Journal*, (1842) 71; *Times* (London), 19
Niagara Escarpment, 19, 21, 26, 28, 30, 31, 32, 33, 34, 37, 48, 50, 101, 138, 139
Niagara River, 31
Niagara-on-the-Lake, 128
Norris (James) Mills, 56, 58

Oak Hill, 99
Ontario Paper Co., 67

Petersburg, 109
Phelps, Noah, 120; Phelps' Machine, 36, 44, 45
Pick Leeson Park, 139
Pilot Boats, 80
Port Colborne, 24, 25, 35, 37, 38, 62, 65, 66, 68, 70, 73, 74, 76, 79, 80, 82, 94, 109, 110, 111, 120, 121, 122, 123, 124, 129, 136, 138, 142, 143; Port Colborne Historical and Marine Museum, 154
Port Dalhousie, xii, 23, 52, 62, 64, 65, 69, 70, 73, 75, (ca. 1878) 93, 95, 100, 109, 114, 116, 117, 118, 119, 124, 140, (ca. 1880) 141, 150, 154, 156, 157; Port Dalhousie Quorum, 155
Port Maitland, 24
Port Robinson, 25, 34, 36, 64, 72, 73, 77, 106, 107, 131, 142, 144
Port Weller, 33, 38, 54, 65, 74, 77, 80, 83, 89, 90, 91, 95, 100, 129, 130, 141; Port Weller Drydocks, 74
Provincial Paper Co., (ca. 1920) 64

Queenston Heights, Battle of, 22

Raceways, 37, 39, 42, 56, 58, 60, 64, 106, 133
Railroads/Railways, 40, 50, 90, 144; Algoma Central Railway, 65; Canada Southern Railway, 135; Canadian National Railway, 111, 145; Grand Trunk Railway, 38, 40, 50, 58, 62, 66, 70, 73, 82, 148; London and Birmingham Railway (Eng.), 86; Niagara, St. Catharines and Toronto Railway, 64, 65, 117; Welland Railway, 50, 62, 64, 73, 99, 101, 104
Ramey's Bend, 83
Recreation and Sports, 116-125, 121, 129, 156; *see also* Royal Canadian Henley Regatta
Rehabilitate the Old Feeder Canal Association, 154
Riordon, John, 61; Riordon Pulp and Paper, 61
Riverside Mill, 35
Robertson Bros. foundry workers, 96
Robinson, Hon. John Beverley, 24, 25, 107
Rodman Hall, 149
Royal Canadian Henley Regatta, 118, 119
Royal Commission on Inland Navigation, 1871, 50

Sabotage, 136
St. Catharines, xi, 20, (ca. 1823) 21, 32, (ca. 1871) 39, (ca. 1862) 43, 46, 47, 52, 57, (ca. 1890) 58, (ca. 1890) 62, (ca. 1880) 63, (ca. 1885) 68, 69, (ca. 1864) 71, (1874) 72, (1880) 75, 77, 84, 87, (ca. 1857) 96, (ca. 1925) 97, 99, 109, 121, 124, 134, 135, 139, 145, 149, 152, 154, 156
St. Catharines Historical Museum, 46, 101, 153; St. Catharines Centennial Logo, 98
St. Catherine of Alexandria (R.C. Cathedral), 87
St. Johns, 128
St. Lawrence Seaway Authority, 96, 140, 156; St. Lawrence Seaway Headquarters, 97
St. Paul Street (St. Catharines), (ca. 1885) 68
Scots on the Welland Canal, 48, 84
Select Committee of Legislature (Upper Canada), 1825, 43
Settlements, 99-102; *see also* under individual names
Seven Mile Stake (Welland), 104
Shipbuilding and shipbuilders: Abbey's Shipyard, 73;

Anderson (ship-builder), 72; Andrew's Dockyard, 64, 69; Armington, Russell, 72; Beatty, Matthew, 73, 82; Hardison, George, 73, 75; Ross, William, 73; Simpson, Melancthon, 72, 73, 75; Upper, James, 106; White, Alfred, 73; [Louis] Shickluna's Shipyard, 56, 69, **71, 72**

Shipman, Paul, 20, 21, 98; Shipman's Corners, **98**

Ships: ii, ix, 43, 50, 52, 56, 62, 64, 65, 66, 71-84, **83**, 118; ALGOWAY, 115; ANNIE AND JANE, xi, xii, 123, **154, 155**; ANNIE PETERSON (schooner), **77**; ARK, **75**; ARTHUR STOVE, **131**; AUGUSTA, **77**; BLUENOSE, **113**; BRITANNIA (Royal Yacht), **116**; CANADIAN CENTURY (laker), **77**; CITY OF ST. CATHARINES (steamer), **73**; DALHOUSIE CITY, **116**; DREDGE PRIMROSE, **82**; EMERALD (barque), **75**; EMPRESS OF INDIA, **62**; ENERGY FREEDOM (barge), **80, 81**; ERIE BELLE, **107**; FURIA, **132**; GARDEN CITY, **117**; JAMES McWHIRTER, **73**; LA CANADIENNE, **131**; LEMOYNE, 76, **123**; MAJESTIC (tug), **81**; (H.M.C.S.) NIPIGON, **114**; ORIOLE, **70**; PEARL, **122**; PERSIA, 58, **75**; PIC RIVER, **58**; QU'APPELLE (pilot boat), **80**; R.H. BROUGHTON, **xii**, 123; SANTA MARIA, **114**; SCOTT MISENER (laker), **83**; STEELTON, **130**; STONEFAX, **131**; TADOUSSAC, **151**; UC-97 (German submarine, 1917), **123**; VANDALIA, **46**

Ship types: Barges, 78, 80; Canallers, 43, 74; Dredges, 73, 80, **82**; Scows, 78, 79; Shunters, 78, 90; Tugs, 73, 78

Slabtown (Merritton), 61, 87, 101

Statistics, Appendix, 159

Steam Power, **48**

Stephenson House, 71, 98

Stoneboats, 37, 48, 49

Strachan, John, 25

Stumptown, 102

Syphon Culverts, 36, 124, 142, **143**

Taylor and Bate's Brewery, 56, 63, 71, 97, 98

Thomas, J.H., 54

Thorold, **ii**, (1882) viii, 33, 40, 41, 53, 54, (1932) 55, 58, **59**, 64, (ca. 1910) 65, 67, 73, 76, 78, 81, 88, 94, **102**, 103, 109, 115, 126, 131, 132, 138, **145**, 148

Thorold, Sir John, M.P. (Eng.), 102; Thorold Mill, **59**

Tools and Engineering Equipment, 36, 37, 38, 43, **44**, 48, 49, **50**, 53, 78, 85, 88, 90

Towboys, **viii, xi, xv**, 56, 63, 93, 102

Towpaths, 140

Town Hall (Merritton), **101**

Tunnels, 35, 36, 37, 40, 142, 148

Twelve Mile Creek, 19, 20, 58, 60, 62, 63, 70, 71, 72, 98, 116, 117, 139, 140

United Empire Loyalists, 22, 87, 98

Urbanization, 85-98

Van Wyck and Johnson (Lumber and Planing Mill), (ca. 1876) **61**

Wainfleet, 113

Water Pollution, 64, 68, 133, 134; *see also* Lampreys

Water Power, 19, 42, 56, 60, 64, **65**, 133; Water Supply, 34, 35, 37, 60, 64, 133, **139**

Weirs and Ponds, 18, 37, **41**, 71, 118, 119, 139

Welland (City), 34, 35, 36, 49, **61**, 65, 73, (ca. 1890) **104**, 105, 109, 114, **121**, 125, 135, **142**, 144

Welland By-Pass, 18, **105**, 124, **142**

Welland Canal: First, x, xi, xii, xiii, 18, 24, 28, 29, 40, 42, 46, 56, 57, 84, 106, 107, 128, **133**, 140, 140, 158, 159; Second, xiii, 18, 28, 30, 32, 34, 39, 43, 46, 47, 48, 51, 52, 56, 58, 60, 61, 62, 63, 64, 65, 68, 70, 71, 87, 92, 93, 96, 98, 101, 102, 103, 106, 107, 109, 120, 134, 135, 136, 140, 141, 142, 144, 149, 153, 154, 156, 158, 159; Third, viii, xiii, 18, 28, 32, 34, 35, 36, 38, 39, 40, 41, 48, 49, 50, 52, 53, 62, 64, 67, 68, 70, 73, 75, 100, 101, 102, 103, 104, 109, 112, 114, 116, 117, 119, 120, 121, 122, 123, 124, 125, 128, 129, 131, 137, 138, 140, 142, 144, 145, 148, 150, 158, 159; Fourth, ii, ix, xiii, 18, 28, 33, 36, 37, 38, 39, 51, 53, 55, 60, 68, 76, 88, 90, 92, 94, 95, 96, 103, 105, 106, 111, 113, 114, 116, 121, 124, 126, 130, 131, 132, 141, 142, 145, 146, 147, 148, 158, 159

Welland Canal Company, xiii, xvi, 20, 24, **25**, 44, 46, 59, 60, 82, 84, 106, 142

Welland Canal Field Battery, **136**, 137

Welland Canal Parkway Board, 156; Welland Canals Foundation, 155

Welland Canals Preservation Association, 153, **156**, 157; Welland Canals Society, 155, **156**

Welland Mill, **103**; Welland River, 34, 35, 113, 142, **143**

Welland Vale Manufacturing Co., **62**; Welland Vale Wharf, 116

Weller Block (Welland), 104

Wellington, 1st Duke of (Wellesley, Arthur), **xvi-xvii**, 25

Wells, Col. Joseph, 24

Whitman Barnes Manufacturing Co., **156**

Willson Carbide, 64

Wood House Hotel, (1877) **100**

World War I (1914-1918), 51, 136, **137**; World War II (1939-1945), 123

Yates, J. Barentse, 99; Yates Street (St. Catharines), 71, 97, **99**

ROBERTA M. STYRAN received her early education in Fredericton, New Brunswick, her B.A. and M.A. from McMaster University in Hamilton, Ontario, and her Ph.D. from the University of Toronto. From 1967 to 1978 she lectured in Medieval History at Brock University in St. Catharines, Ontario. During that time she became fascinated with the history of the Welland Canal and began her collaboration with Dr. Taylor. A founding director of the Welland Canals Preservation Association, she also served on the board of the St. Catharines Historical Museum. Since 1980 she has lived in Toronto, doing free-lance research, writing and editing – and visiting canal and industrial revolution sites in Great Britain. She is currently on the boards of the Ontario Society for Industrial Archaeology and the Canadian Canals Society, and acts as consultant for the Welland Canals Society.

ROBERT R. TAYLOR was born and raised in Victoria, B.C. He received his B.A. and M.A. at the University of British Columbia and his Ph.D. at Stanford University in California. Since 1966 he has lived in St. Catharines, Ontario, where he is Associate Professor of History at Brock University. He is the author of *The Word in Stone. The Role of Architecture in the National Socialist Ideology* (University of California Press, 1974) and *Hohenzollern Berlin. Construction and Reconstruction* (P.D. Meany Publishers, 1985). In the field of local Niagara history, he has published *Discovering St. Catharines Heritage* (St. Catharines L.A.C.A.C., 1980) and *Our Great Age of Destruction* (St. Catharines Historical Society, 1985). He was also a co-founder of the Welland Canals Preservation Association in 1978 and served as a director for three years. He was active for another three years on the St. Catharines Local Architecture Conservation Committee and was the first secretary of the Canadian Canal Society for several years after its founding in 1982.

Together, **Dr. Styran** and **Dr. Taylor** have co-produced several synchronized slide-tape presentations, three of which were for the Welland Canals Preservation Association. This work led to their booklet, *How to Produce Your Own Audio-Visual Show* (1982), for the Ontario Historical Society's series "Approaching Ontario's Past." They have also co-authored "The Welland Canal: Creator of a Landscape," *Ontario History*, LXXII, no. 4 (December 1980); "The Past and Future of the Old Welland Canals," *The Welland Canals. Proceedings of the First Annual Niagara Peninsula History Conference* (Brock University, 1979); and "Purges, Prosperity and Doorian's Pizzeria," *Immigration and Settlement in the Niagara Peninsula. Proceedings of the Third Annual Niagara Peninsula History Conference* (Brock University, 1981). The latter two articles were based on audio-visual presentations and field trips prepared for the conferences.

John N. Jackson, B.A. (Birmingham), Ph.D. (Manchester) is Professor of Geography at Brock University. He is the author of *The Canadian City: Space – Form – Quality* (1973); *Welland and the Welland Canal: The Welland Canal By-Pass* (1975); *St. Catharines, Ontario. Its Early Years* (1976); *Railways in the Niagara Peninsula* (1978, with John Burtniak); and *The Welland Canals. A Comprehensive Guide* (1982, with Fred A. Addis). He has been active with the Welland Canals Foundation.

Robert F. Legget, O.C., F.R.S.C., is one of Canada's foremost authorities on canals. Born in Liverpool, he graduated in Civil Engineering from Liverpool University (B.A., 1925; M.E., 1927). He worked for several years in heavy engineering in Britain before coming to Canada where, during a multi-faceted professional career, he taught Civil Engineering at Queen's University (1936-38) and the University of Toronto (1938-47). From 1947 until 1969 he was director of the National Research Council's Division of Building Research. He has written several books, including *Rideau Waterway* (1955), *Ottawa Waterway* (1975), and *Canals of Canada* (1976, in the "Canals of the World" series). He is the recipient of numerous awards and honorary degrees.